'The entrance door to Australia':
Australia and East Timor
before the Second World War

# 'The entrance door to Australia':
## *Australia and East Timor*
## *before the Second World War*

*Justin Corfield*

CENTEXT PUBLICATIONS
2015

Gentext Publications
An imprint of Corfield and Company

This edition first published in Australia, 2015
by Gentext Publications
59 Smeaton Close, Lara, Victoria, 3212, Australia

Author: Corfield, Justin J., author.

Title: 'The entrance door to Australia':
Australia and East Timor before the Second World War
/ Justin Corfield.

ISBN: 978 1 876586 27 0 (hardback)

# CONTENTS

# FOREWORD

This is a story that should be told.

The story that led to the landing of Australian troops on the shores of East Timor on the 17th December 1941. A landing opposed by the then neutral Portuguese Government but later accepted by the Timorese people.

The Timorese people paid a heavy price for the battle between Japan and the Allied forces on their soil. This would be the pattern for many years to come. From the invasion by Indonesia in 1975 to the Independence vote in 1999. Over a quarter of the Timorese people perished in these successive encounters.

But this book also documents the Australia /East Timor relationship before these events. From oil exploration to the potential for the sale of East Timor to another power, more likely Australia.

This of course never eventuated, but what did occur was in some quarters a recognition of the strategic importance of East Timor in our region.

Justin Corfield has done an outstanding job of telling this story in the most comprehensive account yet.

It should be on the reading list for every secondary school in Australia. Then, our understanding of the newly independent nation of East Timor, one of our nearest neighbours, would be better understood and appreciated.

Hon Steve Bracks AC
*Premier of Victoria 1999 to 2007*
*Governance Adviser to Former Timor-Leste*
*Prime Minister Kay Rala Xanana Gusmão*

# INTRODUCTION*

At about 2.15 am on 8th December 1941 the Japanese launched their assault on the beaches near Kota Bharu in British Malaya. Seventy minutes later Japanese planes started bombing the American fleet at Pearl Harbor, Hawaii. That same day Shanghai, Hong Kong, Manila and Singapore were also attacked, and the Pacific War had begun. With the Japanese forming a bridgehead at Kota Bharu, and the British planned counter-attack, code-named Operation Matador, in tatters, on 16th December the British evacuated Penang island, an operation that not only demoralised the Allied soldiers fighting the Japanese, but also, owing to the preference given to Europeans in the evacuation, resulted in widespread ethnic tensions that remained throughout the rest of the seventy-day Malayan Campaign.

The retreat from Penang was highly symbolic. It was the British withdrawal from their longest-held colonial possession in Southeast Asia. As

---

\*      For the early history of the island I have used C R Boxer, 'Portuguese Timor: a rough island story, 1515–1960', *History Today* Vol 10, no 5 1960, pp. 349–55; James Dunn, *Timor: a people betrayed*, Sydney: ABC Books, 2001; Geoffrey C Gunn, *Timor Loro Sae: 500 years*, Macau: Livros do Oriente, 1999; and Katherine Georgina Davidson, The Portuguese Colonisation of Timor: the final stage 1850–1912, PhD Thesis, University of New South Wales 1995; Christopher Wray, *Timor 1942: Australian Commandos at war with the Japanese,* Melbourne: Hutchinson, 1987. On the war see Christopher Wray's book; also Henry P Frei, 'Japan's reluctant decision to occupy Portuguese Timor, 1 January 1942–20 February 1942', *Australian Historical Studies* Vol 27, no 107 (1996), pp. 281–302; and Nicholas Tarling, 'Britain, Portugal and East Timor in 1941', *Journal of Southeast Asian Studies* Vol 27, no 1 (1996), pp. 132–38. The idea for this volume came from Michael S Wong to whom I am grateful for some of the early research.

2

the rapidity of the Japanese advance struck fear into both the British and Australian governments, on the following day, 17th December 1941, a joint Australian and Dutch military force moved into the small and 'sleepy' town of Dili to take control of Portuguese East Timor – an overseas province of Portugal. It could have been seen as an act of war with allied soldiers forcing entry into a part of a neutral country, but the Portuguese, Britain's 'oldest ally', restricted themselves to diplomatic manoeuvres and political shadow-boxing, partly on account of the diplomatic skills of Sir Ronald Campbell, British Ambassador to Lisbon. The official reasons given were the deployment of Japanese submarines close to Timor as well as the risk that it might become a Japanese base.[1]

Since the fall of France to Nazi Germany in June 1940, the Portuguese premier, António de Oliviera Salazar, had admired the British determination to fight on, and although Portugal remained neutral throughout the entire Second World War, it leaned towards the Allies. Indeed in 1940 the Duke of Kent had visited Lisbon for the celebrations marking the 800th anniversary of Portugal as a nation.[2]

The anniversary celebrated the date in 1140 when Portugal had gained its independence with the help of English Crusaders who stormed Lisbon. This connection between Portugal and England, remembered in 1940, was not lost on the small but influential British community in Lisbon and its business and social connections in Portuguese society. Historically, Portugal had feared Spain, and the support of English and British soldiers over centuries had helped them on many occasions, notably during the Peninsular War when Napoleon had placed his brother on the throne of Spain and invaded Portugal in 1807.

Although the neutrality of Portugal ensured that its other African and Asian possessions remained untouched, the joint Australian-Dutch move into East Timor was to lead directly to the Japanese invasion on 20th February 1942. The Japanese then occupied East Timor until September 1945.

On 2nd December 1941, before hostilities with Japan had broken out[3], the Australian government, worried about the possibility of an impending

[1]   From a statement issued by the Information Bureau of the Government of the Netherlands East Indies, published in *The Times* 19 December 1951, p. 4.
[2]   Tom Gallagher, 'Anglo-Portuguese relations since 1900', *History Today* (June 1986), p. 43.
[3]   Excluding, of course, the conflict in China.

war with Japan, had already noted the strategic importance of Portuguese Timor:

> It is essential that in the event of Japanese attack on this territory, Britain should declare war irrespective of United States' attitude. Portuguese Timor is the entrance door to Australia... We think a definite understanding with Portugal should now be negotiated upon this footing.[4]

Before 1941 there had been limited but important links between Australia and East Timor. This volume seeks to outline some of these connections.

---

[4]    *Documents on Australian Foreign Policy*, Canberra: AGPS, 1998, Vol 5, p. 263.

R. Brings, Makassar.    Inboorlingen van Timor.

People in Dili in the 1890s.

Passar te Timor Dilly

The market in Dili.

# CHAPTER ONE

The island of Timor had long been a source of sandalwood for the great trading entrepot of Malacca for many years before the Portuguese captured the port of Malacca in 1511, and it was from this new base in the Malacca Strait, the Portuguese themselves sailed to Timor and established contact with the island. The *Suma Oriental* by Portuguese official Tomé Pires mentions Timor in 1515, and there is a possibility that a mission by Jorge Fogasa from Malacca went to Timor in 1516 – that is the date traditionally given for the foundation of the township of Dili which was to become the Portuguese administrative centre for the island. But the first Europeans who definitely went to Timor were the crew of the *Victoria* of Ferdinand Magellan – Magellan having been killed in the Philippines some nine months earlier. A brief account of the island by the *Victoria*'s historian Antonio Pigafetta, survives. It describes some trade between the Spanish and the locals at Amabau, near the modern-day township of Batugede. Master Andrew, one of the gunners on the ship, was English, and therefore was the first recorded Englishman to visit what is now East Timor.

In 1566 some Portuguese Dominican friars from Malacca built a fort on the island of Solor, just north of Timor, to protect themselves and their local converts. However the fort did not remain Portuguese for long. It was attacked and captured by the Dutch in 1613 – the Portuguese and the Dutch battled for control of the island for the next thirty years. As a result the Portuguese decided to establish a base on the north-west coast of the island of Timor. It has long been argued, particularly persuasively by Kenneth McIntyre in his *The Secret Discovery of Australia* (1977), that some of the Portuguese during the sixteenth century, presumably from bases in Timor, probably also visited Australia. Indeed one of the earliest people connected with both Timorese and Australian history is Manuel Godinho de Erédia (1563–1623), the first person, chronologically[5], to have a place in the *Australian Dictionary of Biography*. Mention of East Timor is also made by English merchant Ralph Fitch[6]; and also by English sea captain John Saris.

Most of the European contact with Timor remained restricted to the trade in sandalwood, and used it as a source for slaves. It was from this period a number of Portuguese *topasse* communities grew from descendants of Portuguese sailors, some other European traders, and local women. Some sailors also began to make a new home for themselves in Timor. In 1580, with the death of the Portuguese King Henry, Philip II, the King of Spain, acceded to the Portuguese throne, and Portugal and Spain were merged, although Philip was careful to ensure that the Portuguese retained autonomy. However with Spain being involved in conflicts in the Netherlands, it was not long before the Dutch turned their attention to attacking the Spanish or the Portuguese colonial possessions.

When the Dutch started threatening Portuguese Malacca during the 1630s, the Portuguese, fearing losing control of the profitable trade throughout Southeast Asia, not only reinforced the defences at Malacca, but also bolstered them at many of the other Portuguese trading stations throughout Southeast Asia. They built a fort at Kupang in West Timor in 1640, which seems to be the first European defensive position on the island. In the following year these Portuguese fears were proven correct when the Dutch did attack, and later capture, Malacca and the Portuguese were forced to concentrate their energies in the region around Timor.

Just before the Dutch attacks, the Portuguese had sent over soldiers from Portugal, to protect their possessions. In time of attack, these men would be supported by local people and crew from visiting Portuguese ships to form quite an adequate defence. Some of soldiers married locally, but many did not, and were isolated a little from the 'locals'. This can be clearly

---

[5]    Pedro de Quiros is listed as having been born in '1563?', presumably because he was about the same age as de Erédia.

[6]    Michael Edwardes, *Ralph Fitch, Elizabethan in the Indies*, London: Faber, 1972, p. 93 & 157.

seen after the fall of Malacca with the local Portuguese community allowed to remain but the soldiers were moved by the Dutch to a site just south of Batavia where they lived as a distinct group for many years.

When the Dutch captured Kupang in 1653, the Portuguese, through a series of alliances with local rulers, managed to continue to exert control over much of the rest of the island. It seems that the Portuguese and some of the Timorese then harassed the newcomers. This left the Dutch with a small base that had to be reinforced by sea. After some small wars with the Dutch, the Portuguese began to focus on the eastern half of the island, leaving the Dutch in the west. In 1661 a treaty was signed between the Dutch and the Portuguese but the rule of both the Dutch and Portuguese remained precarious for the next 150 years with both sides suspecting the other, and also any other Europeans in the region, of harbouring colonial ambitions. When William Dampier sailed to Timor in 1699 the Dutch treated him with great caution, suspecting him of being a spy, and actually accusing him of being a pirate.

William Dampier

During the Napoleonic Wars the rulers of both Portugal and the Netherlands fled overseas as Napoleon invaded both countries. As a result, the British occupied West Timor, to safeguard it from French depredations. The British seemed to have done little there other than building the army barracks at Kupang in about 1810[7] and destroy much of the local archives, apparently using the paper they found in the Kupang archives for their gun cartridges.[8] Samuel Garmston, later a Captain in the Royal Marines, and later still a Major-General, is recorded as having been involved in the taking of Fort Kupang in 1814.[9]

The grave of Samuel Garmston.
Courtesy Sally Lloyd.

---

[7]     Bernard Callinan, *Independent Company*, London: Heinemann, 1953, p. 9.

[8]     Victor Crittenden, *A bibliography of the First Fleet*, Canberra: Australian National University, 1981, p. 66.

[9]     H G Hart, *The Annual Army List and Militia List for 1860*, London: John Murray, 1860, p. 24. He was born in 1787 at St Nicholas, Worcester, and in 1851 was living at St Johns, Alverstoke, near Gosport, Hampshire. He died on 15th November 1859, aged 72, and was buried in the churchyard at St Bartholomew, Grindley, Worcestershire. Buried with him in the same grave are John Garmston who died on 17th February 1867, aged 77; Mary Ann Garmston, who died on 8th December 1854, aged 70; and Susanna Garmston, who died on 24th July 1875, aged 82.

West Timor was returned to the Dutch at the end of the wars and a precarious state of low-level hostility remained between the Portuguese and the Dutch. Treaties in 1859 and in 1893 (the Lisbon Convention) helped resolve the boundaries between the two sides – although the latter treaty only came into force in 1914. This left the western part of the island in Dutch hands and the eastern part, as well as an enclave around the port of Pante Macassar (now Okussi), in Portuguese hands.

A number of the early explorers of Australia seem to have visited Timor, but these visits were largely restricted to West Timor. William Dampier (1652– 1715) left a short account of Kupang, as did William Bligh who was cast adrift from the HMS *Bounty*. Bligh, following the mutiny on his ship, was at sea for six weeks in an open boat with his loyal supporters. He managed to navigate 3,618 miles (without maps), reaching Timor on 12th June 1789 – just seventeen months after the First Fleet reached Sydney Cove. When Bligh and his men saw Timor, as the men were without maps, there was a discussion about where the nearest settlement was, and Bligh seemed to remember that Kupang was on the south-west corner of the island, rather than on the north coast as others remembered it, and hence they made for Kupang arriving on 14th June in a rather emaciated state. From Kupang, while all the men rested, Bligh did wrote home to his wife. The letter was presumedly sent on the next ship heading to Europe – the first reference to a letter to England sent from Timor. In it he described what had befallen the *Bounty*. Bligh was later to become governor of New South Wales.

When news of the mutiny on the *Bounty* (since made famous by numerous books and several films), reached the Admiralty in London, the Royal Navy despatched the HMS *Pandora* to catch the mutineers who were led by Fletcher Christian. On 17th September 1791 Captain Edward Edwards arrived in Kupang. As with Bligh, he did not have his ship.[10] Edwards had sailed for Tahiti, and had managed to capture some of the mutineers there. However, after sailing in the Pacific, the *Pandora* had floundered on the Great Barrier Reef and went down with 35 men on 29th August 1791. Edwards, the surviving crew and some of the mutineers who had managed to swim to the life rafts – some 120 altogether – reached Kupang.

Edwards and his men and prisoners, when they arrived at Kupang made immediate contact with the Dutch authorities. The Dutch had no news of

---

[10] For a detailed account of the *Pandora*, see Luis Marden, 'Wreck of HMS Pandora', *National Geographic Magazine* Vol 168, no 4 (October 1985), pp. 422– 51.

Fletcher Christian but they did hand over to them eight adults and two children who had arrived in Kupang three months earlier, on 5th June, claiming to be survivors of a shipwreck on the Australian coast. The Dutch thought they might have something to do with the mutiny on the *Bounty*, and had watched them closely refusing to let them leave. It rapidly emerged that they were, in fact, escaped convicts from Sydney Cove, five being from the First Fleet: William and Mary Bryant, James Martin, James Cox and Samuel Bird. This group had made the 3,254 miles voyage from Sydney to Timor where they hoped for better treatment than that they had received as convicts in New South Wales.

The ex-convicts were handed over to Captain Edwards when he arrived, and then put on board the *Rembang*, a Dutch East Indiaman, which took the Britons – the men from the *Pandora*, the captured mutineers from the *Bounty*, and the new prisoners, to Batavia (Jakarta). William Bryant died in Batavia; Cox and Bird died near the Cape of Good Hope; but Mary Bryant and James Martin were taken back to England – Mary's plight so touched James Boswell, the London biographer and raconteur, that he put her up in his house before she returned to her family in Cornwall. Mary Bryant's life has subsequently been the subject of many books but none of the authors have been able to track down what became of her.

Yet another ship arrived at Timor in similarly distressing circumstances. John Arscott from Cornwall had been transported to Sydney for theft. Commended for saving a ship sailing to Norfolk Island, he discovered that his term of transportation had already expired before he received his pardon. In 1791 Arsott sailed to British India to get supplies; and in April 1793 he left for England with his wife, Catherine (née Prior), also a First Fleeter who had actually been convicted of highway robbery with Mary Bryant (née Braund) and another woman. However in July when the ships on which they were travelling were on Tate Island in the Torres Strait to take on fresh water, the shore party was attacked by local people who had seemed friendly. The ships left thinking that the entire group had been killed although John Arscott and two others survived. Arscott and his companions headed for Timor in their small boat. After ten days at sea – they had few supplies – they landed on another island and from there managed to board a trading vessel to Banda and Batavia.[11]

[11] Information drawn from Mollie Gillen, *The Founders of Australia*, North Sydney: Library of Australian History, 1989; Robert Hughes, *The Fatal Shore*, London: Collins Harvill, 1987; and *Australian Dictionary of Biography*. For further information see Charles H Currey, *The transportation, escape and pardoning of*

However not all the Britons to arrive on Timor during this period were in distress, although the *Santa Maria* was to be lost off the coast of Timor in 1812. Hydrographer John McCluer, mapping out the region for the British East India Company called at Timor in 1792 – his maps were to be crucial to Matthew Flinders when he sailed to the region eleven years later. In September 1793 the *Chesterfield* (Commander William Brampton) sailed from Norfolk Island to Timor – Brampton Island, in the Whitsundays, being names after the commander.[12] There was also some sandalwood trade between Timor and Batavia, on British ships, in the late 1790s with ships ensuring they sailed via Timor.[13] When the Australian navigator Matthew Flinders also called at Timor in May 1803, he found many ships there in search of sea-slugs. One of his crew, William Westall, made at least two drawings of Timor. By this time the discovery of sandalwood in Fiji had begun to affect the trade with Timor and hence Timor's importance.[14]

The other great saga of the period which involved both Australia and Timor was when Thomas Braidwood Wilson, a medical doctor, was shipwrecked in 1829 in Torres Strait. Wilson and the surviving crew managed to row about 1,000 miles to Timor, and from there visited the Swan River with Wilson's account of Perth being one of the first of the settlement which had been founded earlier the same year.

It is interesting to note that in the settlement of Australia, the inland western boundary of New South Wales was left deliberately vague at the time of initial settlement. Part of this, and its later establishment at 135 degrees east was apparently to ensure that New South Wales would keep a 'respectful distance' from East Timor and thereby not antagonise Portugal, Britain's oldest ally.[15]

---

*Mary Bryant*, Sydney: Angus & Robertson 1963; Frederick Albert Pottle, *Boswell and the Girl from Botany Bay*, London: Heinemann, 1938; and the novel, Geoffrey Rawson, *The strange case of Mary Bryant*, London: Robert Hale, 1938.
[12] The journal of the *Chesterfield* is held in the Blechynden Papers at the British Museum, London. An abridged version of Brampton's journal was published by Matthew Flinders in *A Voyage to Terra Australia*, London 1814, Vol 1.
[13] Margaret Steven, *Merchant Campbell 1769–1846*, Melbourne: Oxford University Press, 1965, p. 30.
[14] Lyndon Rose, *Richard Siddins of Port Jackson*, Roebuck Books: Canberra, 1984, p. 57 & 89.
[15] Bill Gammage, 'Early boundaries of New South Wales', *Historical Studies* Vol 19, No 77 (1981), pp. 524–31.

Alfonse Pellion, *Our first disembarkation on Timor*, c.1819

Two Frenchmen François Péron (1775–1810) and Charles Lesseur (1778–1846) both went to Timor in 1803 to hunt crocodiles.[16] Louis-Claude Desaules de Freycinet (1779–1842), the French cartographer who sailed with Nicolas Baudin in Australian waters, visited Timor in 1818, leaving an interesting description of West Timor.[17] Freycinet's wife, Rose, left a journal in which she described East Timor:

Upon our arrival in Timor, Louis made me promise not to eat any manner of fruit. In spite of temptation, I kept my promise. I was only allowed to eat mangoes, a fruit which I cannot compare to any other which we have in France, because they are not as refreshing...

November 1818 – The length and difficulties of our voyage during the last month or so, together with the number of sick crewmen and the

---

[16] See Anne Lombard-Jourdan, 'François Péron and Charles Lesueur a Timor: une chasse au crocadile en 1803', *Archipel* No 54 (1997), pp. 81–121.
[17] Originally published as *Voyage autour du monde*, Paris 1844, and English language edition, *Reflections on New South Wales 1788–1839*, was published in 2001.

fact that we had not been able to take on enough supplies at Kupang, all combined to persuade the Commander to call at Dili...

We anchored four days ago... The Portuguese Governor, Don José Pinto Alcoforado d'Azavedo e Souza, welcomed the dear Commander and his crew with truly remarkable courtesy... he sent me fruit and fresh bread together with an invitation to dine with him the next day. To this end, he announced to my husband that all the notable women of the colony would be gathered at his home to receive me.[18]

Some of the early visitors to Timor from Australia during this period were intrigued by Timor's botany: Ferdinand Bauer painted plants there in the 1800s, and Robert Brown, travelling with Flinders, collected 200 species of plants from Timor. Allan Cunningham painted Timorese plants in 1818 and John Richardson, a gardener and convict who, after being freed, was sent to Dutch Timor in 1826 to bring plants and seeds to Sydney. Haphazard contact continued for many years. The *Tuscan* (Captain T Stavers), a whaler, called in at Timor in the 1830s and an account of their time there is preserved at the Royal Geographical Society.

John Boultbee, from Bunny, Nottinghamshire, England, had spent some time in the West Indies where he had planned to become a plantation manager. However he disliked the treatment of the slaves and migrated to Van Diemen's Land (Tasmania) with his brother and then worked as a sealer. In January 1833 he visited Timor – two years later he wrote his 'Journal of a rambler' in Ceylon where he settled. His early description of New Zealand merits him an important place in early New Zealand history, and the manuscript account of his time in Timor is held at the Alexander Turnbull Library, Wellington, being edited and published in 1986.

In October 1839 Judah Solomon, nephew of Emanuel Solomon, a convict who was to become an important South Australian merchant and later politician, brought a supply of Timorese ponies to sell in Adelaide. It is not recorded whether these were from Dutch or Portuguese Timor, although given the description by Wallace (see below), they might well have been

---

[18]     Rose de Freycinet, *A woman of courage: the journal of Rose de Freycinet on her voyage around the world 1817–1820*, translated and edited by Marc Serge Rivière, Canberra: National Library of Australia, 1996, p. 59.

from the latter. John Lort Stokes, later Admiral in the Royal Navy, made a survey of East Timor in 1841.

As Kupang, the main town of Dutch Timor is on the western coast, and Dili, the main town of Portuguese Timor is on the more remote northern coast, many of these early Australian contacts were either definitely with, or appear to be with, Dutch Timor. Therefore when the British naturalist, Lord Alfred Russel Wallace, spent four months in Dili in 1861, his account, much read in Australia, became the standard English-language account of the Portuguese Timor. It was reported 'he found Dili to be a most miserable place. His collecting was poor apart from butterflies. He describes some beautiful swallow-tale butterflies and other varieties of whites and yellows, many of which were quite new to him.'[19] Wallace's complete description follows:

> I arrived at Delli [Dili], the capital of the Portuguese possessions in Timor, on January 12, 1861, and was kindly received by Captain Hart, an Englishman and an old resident, who trades in the produce of the country and cultivates coffee on an estate at the foot of the hills. With him I was introduced to Mr Geach[20], a mining-engineer who had been for two years endeavouring to discover copper in sufficient quantity to be worth working.
>
> Delli is a most miserable place compared with even the poorest of the Dutch towns. The houses are all of mud and thatch; the fort is only a mud inclosure; and the custom-house and church are built of the same mean materials, with no attempt at decoration or even neatness. The whole aspect of the place is that of a poor native town, and there is no sign of cultivation or civilization round about it. His Excellency the Governor's[21] house is the only

---

[19]     John G Wilson, *The forgotten naturalist: in search of Alfred Russel Wallace*, Melbourne: Australian Scholarly Publishing, 2000, p. 156.

[20]     He was from Cornwall and the surname is a common Cornish one, which makes it hard to search for any information on him. The British Museum in London also holds the original of a letter which Wallace wrote from Dili to his brother-in-law Thomas Sims on 15th March 1861, in which he describes Geach as a 'very intelligent and pleasant fellow, but [who] has now left [Timor]'. He later implies that Geach moved to Singapore. James Marchant, *Alfred Russel Wallace: Letters and Reminiscences*, New York: Arno Press, 1975, p. 64 & 157.

[21]     Afonso de Castro, Governor 1859–1863.

one that makes any pretensions to appearance, and that is merely a low white-washed cottage or bungalow. Yet there is one thing in which civilization exhibits itself. Officials in black and white European costume, and officers in gorgeous uniforms, abound in a degree quite disproportionate to the size or appearance of the place.

The town being surrounded for some distance by swamps and mud-flats is very unhealthy, and a single night often gives a fever to new-comers which not unfrequently proves fatal. To avoid this malaria, Captain Hart always slept at his plantation, on a slight elevation about two miles from the town, where Mr Geach also had a small house, which he kindly invited me to share. We rode there in the evening and in the course of two days my baggage was brought up, and I was able to look about me and see if I could do any collecting.

For the first few weeks I was very unwell and could not go far from the house. The country was covered with low spiny shrubs and acacias, except in a little valley where a stream came down from the hills, where some fine trees and bushes shaded the water and formed a very pleasant place to ramble. There were plenty of birds about, and of a tolerable variety of species; but very few of them were gaily coloured. Indeed, with one or two exceptions, the birds of this tropical island were hardly so ornamental as those of Great Britain. Beetles were so scarce that a collector might fairly say there were none…

Early in February we made arrangements to stay for a week at a village called Baliba [Balibo], situated about four miles off on the mountains, at an elevation of 2,000 feet. We took our baggage and a supply of all necessaries on pack-horses; and though the distance by the route we took was not more than six or seven miles, we were half a day getting there. The roads were mere tracks, sometimes up steep rocky stairs, sometimes in narrow gullies worn by the horses' feet, and where it was necessary to tuck up our-legs on our horses' necks to avoid having them crushed. At some of these places the baggage had to be unloaded, at others it was knocked off. Sometimes the ascent or descent was so steep that it was easier to walk than to cling to our ponies' backs; and thus we went up and down, over bare hills whose surface was covered with small pebbles and scattered over with Eucalyti, reminding me of what I had read of parts of the interior of Australia rather than of the Malay Archipelago.

The village consisted of three houses only, with low walls, raised a few feet on posts, and very high roofs thatched with grass hanging down to within two or three feet of the ground. A house which was unfinished and partly open at the back was given for our use, and in it we rigged up a table, some benches, and a screen, while an inner enclosed portion served us for a sleeping apartment. We had a splendid view down upon Delli and the sea beyond. The country round was undulating and open, except in the hollows, where there were some patches of forest, which Mr Geach, who had been all over the eastern part of Timor, assured me was the most luxuriant he had yet seen in the island as in hopes of finding some insects here, but was much disappointed, owing perhaps to the dampness of the climate; for it was not till the sun was pretty high that the mists cleared away, and by noon we were generally clouded up again, so that there was seldom more than an hour or two of fitful sunshine. We searched in every direction for birds and other game, but they were very scarce. On our way I had shot the fine white-headed pigeon, *Ptilonopus cinctus*, and the pretty little lorikeet, *Trichoglossus euteles*. I got a few more of these at the blossoms of the Eucalypti, and also the allied species *Trichoglossus iris*, and a few other small but interesting birds. The common jungle-cock of India (*Gallus bankiva*) was found here, and furnished us with some excellent meals but we could get no deer. Potatoes are grown higher up the mountains in abundance, and are very good. We had a sheep killed every other day, and ate our mutton with much appetite in the cool climate which rendered a fire always agreeable.

Although one-half [of] the European residents in Delli are continually ill from fever, and the Portuguese have occupied the place for three centuries, no one has yet built a house on these fine hills, which, if a tolerable road were made, would be only an hour's ride from the town; and almost equally good situations might be found on a lower level at half an hour's distance. The fact that potatoes and wheat of excellent quality are grown in abundance at from 3,000 to 3,500 feet elevation, shows what the climate and soil are capable of if properly cultivated. From one to two thousand feet high, coffee would thrive; and there are hundreds of square miles of country, over which all the varied products which require climates between those of coffee and wheat would flourish; but no attempt has yet been made to form a single mile of road, or a single acre of plantation!

There must be something very unusual in the climate of Timor to permit wheat being grown at so moderate an elevation. The grain is of excellent quality, the bread made from it being equal to any I have ever tasted; and it is universally acknowledged to be unsurpassed by any made from imported European or American flour. The fact that the natives have (quite of their own accord) taken to cultivating such foreign articles as wheat and potatoes, which they bring in small quantities on the backs of ponies by the most horrible mountain tracks, and sell very cheaply at the sea-side, sufficiently indicates what might be done, if good roads were made, and if the people were taught, encouraged, and protected. Sheep also do well on the mountains; and a breed of hardy ponies in much repute all over the Archipelago, runs half wild; so that it appears as if this island, so barren-looking and devoid of the usual features of tropical vegetation, were yet especially adapted to supply a variety of products essential to Europeans, which the other islands will not produce, and which they accordingly import from the other side of the globe.

On the 24th of February my friend Mr Geach left Timor, having finally reported that no minerals worth working were to be found. The Portuguese were very much annoyed, having made up their minds that copper is abundant, and still believing it to be so. It appears that from time immemorial pure native copper has been found at a place on the coast about thirty miles east of Delli. The natives say they find it in the bed of a ravine, and many years ago a captain of a vessel is said to have got some hundreds-weight of it. Now, however, it is evidently very scarce, as during the two years Mr Geach resided in the Country, none was found. I was shown one piece several pounds' weight, having much the appearance of one of the larger Australian nuggets, but of pure copper instead of gold. The natives and the Portuguese have very naturally imagined, that where these fragments come from there must be more; and they have a report or tradition, that a mountain at the head of the ravine is almost pure copper, and of course of immense value. After much difficulty a company was at length formed to work the copper mountain, a Portuguese merchant of Singapore supplying most of the capital.[22] So confident were they of the existence of the copper, that they thought it would be waste of time and money to have any exploration made first; and accordingly sent to England for a mining-engineer, who was to bring out all necessary tools, machinery, laboratory utensils, a number of mechanics, and stores of all kinds for two years, in order to commence work on a copper-mine which he was told was already discovered. On reaching Singapore a ship was freighted to take the men and stores to Timor, where they at length arrived after much delay, a long voyage, and very great expense.

A day was then fixed to 'open the mines'. Captain Hart accompanied Mr Geach as interpreter. The Governor [Afonso de Castro], the Commandante, the Judge, and all the chief people of the place, went in state to the mountain, with Mr Geach's assistant and some of the workmen. As they went up the valley Mr Geach examined the rocks, but saw no signs of copper. They went on and on, but still nothing except a few mere traces of very poor ore. At length they stood on the copper mountain itself. The Governor stopped, the officials formed a circle, and he then addressed them, saying that at length the day had arrived they had all been so long expecting, when the treasures of the soil of Timor

---

[22]    Possibly the D'Ameidas.

would be brought to light, and much more in very grandiloquent Portuguese; and concluded by turning to Mr Geach, and requesting him to point out the best spot for them to begin work at once, and uncover the mass of virgin copper. As the ravines and precipices among which they had passed, and which had been carefully examined, revealed very clearly the nature and mineral constitution of the country, Mr Geach simply told them that there was not a trace of copper there, and that it was perfectly useless to begin work. The audience were thunderstruck! The Governor could not believe his ears. At length, when Mr Geach had repeated his statement, the Governor told him severely that he was mistaken that they all knew there was copper there in abundance, and all they wanted him to tell them, as a mining-engineer, was how best to get at it ; and that at all events he was to begin work some where. This Mr Geach refused to do, trying to explain, that the ravines had cut far deeper into the hill than he could do in years, and that he would not throwaway money or time on any such useless attempt. After this speech had been interpreted to him, the Governor saw it was no use, and without saying a word turned his horse and rode away, leaving my friends alone on the mountain, They all believed there was some conspiracy that the Englishman would not find the copper, and that they had been cruelly betrayed.

Mr Geach then wrote to the Singapore merchant who was his employer, and it was arranged that he should send the mechanics home again, and himself explore the country for minerals, At first the Government threw obstacles in his way and entirely prevented his moving; but at length he was allowed to travel about, and for more than a year he and his assistant explored the eastern part of Timor, crossing it in several places from sea to sea and ascending every important valley, without finding any minerals that would pay the expense of working. Copper ore exists in several places, but always too poor in quality. The best would pay well if situated in England; but in the interior of an utterly barren country, with roads to make, and all skilled labour and materials to import, it would have been a losing concern. Gold also occurs, but very sparingly and of poor quality. A fine spring of pure petroleum was discovered far in the interior, where it can never be available till the country is civilized. The whole affair was a dreadful disappointment to the Portuguese Government, who had considered It such a certain thing that they had contracted for the Dutch mail steamers to stop at Delli; and several vessels from Australia were induced to come with miscellaneous cargoes, for which they expected to find a ready sale among the population at the newly-opened mines. The lumps of native copper are still, however, a mystery. Mr Geach has examined the country in every direction without being able to trace their origin; so that it seems probable that they result from the debris of old copper-bearing strata, and are not really more abundant than gold nuggets are in Australia or California: A high reward was offered to any native who should find a piece and show the exact spot where he obtained it, but without effect...

The Portuguese government in Timor is a most miserable one. Nobody seems to care the least about the improvement of the country, and at this time, after three hundred years of occupation, there has not been a mile of road made beyond the town, and there is not a solitary European resident anywhere in the interior. All the Government officials oppress and rob the natives as much as they can, and yet there is no care taken to render the town defensible should the Timorese attempt to attack it. So ignorant are the military officers, that having received a small mortar and some shells, no one could be found who knew how to use them; and during an insurrection of the natives (while I was at Delli) the officer who expected to be sent against the insurgents was instantly taken ill! and they were allowed to get possession of all important pass within three miles of the town, where they could defend themselves against ten times the force. The result was that no provisions were brought down from the hills; a famine was imminent, and the Governor had to send off, to beg for supplies from the Dutch Governor of Amboyna.

In its present state Timor is more trouble than profit to its Dutch and Portuguese rulers, and it will continue to be so if unless a different system is pursued; a few good roads into the elevated districts of the interior a conciliatory policy and strict justice towards the natives and the introduction of a good system of cultivation as in Java and Northern Celebes, might yet make Timor a productive and valuable island. Rice grows well on the marshy flats which often fringe the coast, and maize thrives in all the lowlands, and is the common food of the natives as it was when Dampier visited the island in 1699. The small quantity of coffee now grown is of very superior quality, and it might be increased to any extent. Sheep thrive, and would always be valuable as fresh food for whalers and to supply the adjacent islands with mutton, if not for their wool; although it is probable that on the mountains this product might soon be obtained by judicious breeding. Horses thrive amazingly; and enough wheat might be grown to supply the whole Archipelago if there were sufficient inducements to the natives to extend its cultivation, and good roads by which it could be cheaply transported to the coast. Under such a system the natives would soon perceive that European government was advantageous to them. They would begin to save money, and property being rendered secure they would rapidly acquire new wants and new tastes, and become large consumers of European goods.

The next recorded connection between Australia and Timor was in 1864 when Isaac Zachariah, aged 24, married Eva Saunders, aged 17 from London. The marriage took place on 14th May 1864 at Ballarat, with Samuel Herman officiating, and the marriage certificate records that the groom was born in 'Asiatic Timor'.[23]   The couple had one child: Reuben, born in January 1866 (died in March 1866, aged 8 weeks; buried on 6th March at Ballarat Old Cemetery [Section 1, Row 2]). Isaac and Eva appear to have left Victoria soon afterwards. The reason for the reference to *Asiatic* Timor was because there was a Victorian town north-west of Maryborough, which was called Timor, almost certainly named after the island of Timor. There is also Timor Street in the town of Warrnambool, which, according to a local history was also probably named after the island, although no connection between the two is known.[24]

Of the Australians who visited Timor during this period, the most important group were those with Francis Cadell who, in 1867, had the task of locating a site for the capital for the Northern Territory. In this expedition he stopped at Timor (probably once again Dutch Timor). John McKinlay, the explorer, is also recorded as visiting Timor (probably Kupang) in 1866, as did Samuel Sweet in 1870. Dr Henry Forbes, a prominent Scottish naturalist and an honorary fellow of the Geographical Society of Australia, visited Timor in the early 1880s with his wife – their experiences appeared in *A Naturalist's Wanderings in the Eastern Archipelago* (New York 1885). At around this period, three important writers mention Timor. Jules Verne in *Twenty Thousand Leagues Under the Sea* refers to Timorese reverence for ancestral crocodiles; Herman Melville praises whales from Timor in *Moby Dick*, and Joseph Conrad refers to Dili as 'that highly pestilential city' in his novel *Victory*.[25]

For most of the next forty years little is recorded of Australian connections with Timor although in 1887 some Timorese rebelled, killing the governor Alfredo de Lacerda Maia. The rebellion, covered

[23]     Newman Rosenthal, *Formula for Survival: the Saga of the Ballarat Hebrew Congregation*, Hawthorn Press: Melbourne, 1979, p. 21.
[24]     C E Sayers, *By These We Flourish: a history of Warrnambool*, Melbourne: Heinemann, 1969, p. 21.
[25]     References from Ken White, *Criado: a story of East Timor*, Briar Hill, Vic: Indra Publishing, 2002, Chapter 1.

briefly in the world press including the Melbourne *Argus*,[26] was quickly crushed.[27] There was little mention of Timor in Australia until 1912 when there was a rumour that the Portuguese were considering selling their portion of the island to the Germans. In fact these rumours had been circulating around Europe for years.

A Portuguese deputy, Captain José Bento Ferreira d'Almeida, had raised the idea of the sale of Timor, and indeed Mozambique, Guinea, Goa and Macao, in a speech in the Portuguese Cortes (parliament) in June 1891. His suggestion was that Portugal should hold onto São Tomé and Principé, Angola and the Cape Verde islands and sell the rest of Portugal's overseas possessions to reduce the country's public debt.[28] He made the suggestion again in 1900, and being the former Portuguese Minister of Marine, although his idea was rejected by the Portuguese government, it did lead to positive comment in the British press.

Certainly Britain was interested in purchasing the port of Beira in Mozambique through which many exports from Southern Rhodesia and South Africa were taken by railway, for shipping overseas. Although Ferreira d'Almeida's suggestions were rejected by the Portuguese government, there continued to be regular stories in Southern Rhodesia that the Portuguese were interested in selling Beira.[29] There seems to have been, however, little interest in Britain or Australia about the possible sale of Timor. Indeed in 1894 *The Times* reported:

> In the island of Timor imports increased, but exports fell away on account of bad crops. The petroleum wells remain unworked; indeed, the people look with reverence on the burning streams, and believe them to be of divine origin. No steps have been taken to develop the resources of the island; foreigners are not allowed to hold a concession, nor are foreign medical personnel allowed to practise in any Portuguese colony unless provided with a diploma from Lisbon.[30]

---

[26]    Also *The Times*, 11 March 1887, p. 5; 12 March 1887, p. 7.
[27]    To give some idea of the connections between Timor and Lisbon during this period, auctioneers David Feldman of Switzerland, auctioned a letter sent from Dili on 1st December 1886 and which arrived in Lisbon on 26th January 1887, as a 'great rarity', and it was one of the highlights of their sale, *Stamps and Postal History: Europe & Colonies*, Zurich, International Hotel, November 1–5, 1994, lot 20663.
[28]    *The Times*, 9 June 1891, p. 5; 9 September 1902, p. 7.
[29]    Frank Debenham, *Nyasaland: the land of the lake*, London: HMSO, 1955, p. 13.
[30]    *The Times* 29 September 1894, p. 13.

A year later Dutch newspaper in Batavia *Nieuws van den Dag* reported that another insurrection had broken out in East Timor, with rebels defeating troops sent to quell the outbreak. It reported that 'the Secretary and three agents of the Government' had been killed and 'the Governor has left for the interior with reinforcements.'[31]

In 1898 the British and the Germans had drawn up plans for what might happen to Portugal's empire should the opportunity arise. Neither of the countries were actually planning to attack Portugal, but both felt that Portugal might go bankrupt and thus have to divest itself of some of its foreign territories.[32] The secret Anglo-German Agreement of 1898 had assigned East Timor to the Germans (along with northern Angola and northern Mozambique) in the event of a Portuguese withdrawal.

It might not be a coincidence that the Royal Navy vessel HMS *Nelson* was in Kupang during that year. A Midshipman Heath died from the accidental discharge of a gun during this sojourn, resulting in a short mention in the *Queensland Times* in December of that year. In negotiations for a revised agreement between 1911 and 1914 it was decided to give Sao Tomé e Principe to the Germans and Britain would have East Timor should Portugal withdraw.

In contrast the Portuguese government seemed to be entertaining no plans to sell East Timor, or indeed any of their other colonies. On 29th August 1908 the Portuguese Chamber of Peers approved the Convention with the Dutch to agree the border between East and West Timor. However the Dutch opposed some of the border, and the matter was put to international arbitration, leading to the Sentenca Arbitral of April 1913.

---

[31]     *ibid*, 25 September 1895, p. 3.
[32]     Glyn Stone, *The Oldest Ally: Britain and the Portuguese Connection 1936–1941*, London: The Royal Historical Society, 1994, p. 91.

# CHAPTER TWO

In about 1901 an Australian chemist, Dr James Frederick Elliott, later head of Elliott Brothers (later still Elliotts & Australian Drug Ltd of Sydney) was travelling on the steamer *Empire*, when it called in at East Timor. Elliott, born at Balmain in 1858 was the son of a London-born surgeon. A keen yachtsman (he was Rear-Commodore of the Royal Sydney Yacht Club at the time of his sojourn in East Timor), he regularly went overseas to track down new pharmaceutical products.

The *Empire*, under the command of Captain Helms, was taking a large boiler to a location close to Dili. As there was no wharf where Helms could unload the boiler, it was lowered onto a ship's boat. Elliott and some other passengers were watching and noticed that some of the crew, after lighting pipes, threw their matches into the water. Instead of sinking, the matches gave the appearance of floating and soon there were small flames. When Elliott asked Helms about this, Helms told the pharmacist that there was believed to be large concentrations of oil nearby and, in fact, the reason for the boiler being delivered was so that some scientists ashore could try to find the origin of the oil.

Elliott, on his return to Sydney, mentioned this incident to a few of his medical friends and some scientists. Together, in 1902, they subscribed to a share-issue for a company with the purpose of discovering oil on East Timor. This company, largely owned by Elliott and his medical friends, sent an engineer called Alfred Warren and sent him to Timor to bore for oil. On arrival in East Timor, Warren managed to persuade the Portuguese to give him four or five concessions. A small group then established a camp outside Dili – and began work to establish a water supply they drilled holes of about

6-8 foot in depth. These holes filled with a mixture of water and oil encouraging the men in their efforts. As the 1932 Report for Timor Oil Limited noted:

> However they got to work with their boring plant. Very few of those in charge of the work had any expert knowledge of boring for oil, and their plant was not equipped with suitable parts for oil boring. As the bore was driven down to a very shallow depth, there was again an escape of inflammable gas, oil and water. They got down to a depth of three to four hundred feet, with every indication of the presence of petroleum, and at the same time water. Those in charge did not understand the very simple process of cutting off the water so as to secure the oil flow alone.
>
> At any rate the Company muddled along for some seven or eight years without any tangible results. In the meantime, news of what was going on leaked out, and soon the Timor oil field began to be spoken of in circles of keen investors and wealthy capitalists, and shares rose in value.

A surviving postcard sent from Dili to the eight year-old Edward Keith Tolhurst (opposite), dated 13th October 1903, was probably was sent by a member of this exploratory expedition. Keith Tolhurst's father Alfred, was a member of the Melbourne Stock Exchange from 1889 until his death in 1917.[33]

In the meantime, in 1903 the issue of Timor had been raised by a member of the New South Wales Legislative Council. Dr John Creed had been a medical officer on the Cadell expedition to Timor in 1867 and obviously the place had remained in his mind for many years. Writing to the Governor of New South Wales, Sir Harry Rawson, Creed noted the 'especial importance with the [East Timor] territory has to the British Empire is its close proximity to Australia and that it is in a commanding situation with regard to steamers' trading routes between Australian ports, the Philippine Islands and China.'[34]

---

[33]  Keith was educated at Melbourne Grammar School and Felstead, England, serving in the Field Ambulance attached to the 3rd Light Horse in World War I. A member of the Melbourne Stock Exchange from 1917 until 1963, he died on 24th May 1982. *Liber Melburniensis Centenary Edition*, p. 159; *Alumni Felstedienses 1900–1970*, p. 228.

[34]  Details of Creed's memorandum comes from Peter Hastings, 'Timor – some Australian attitudes 1903–1941', in James Cotton (ed), *East Timor & Australia*, Canberra 1999, Chapter 1.

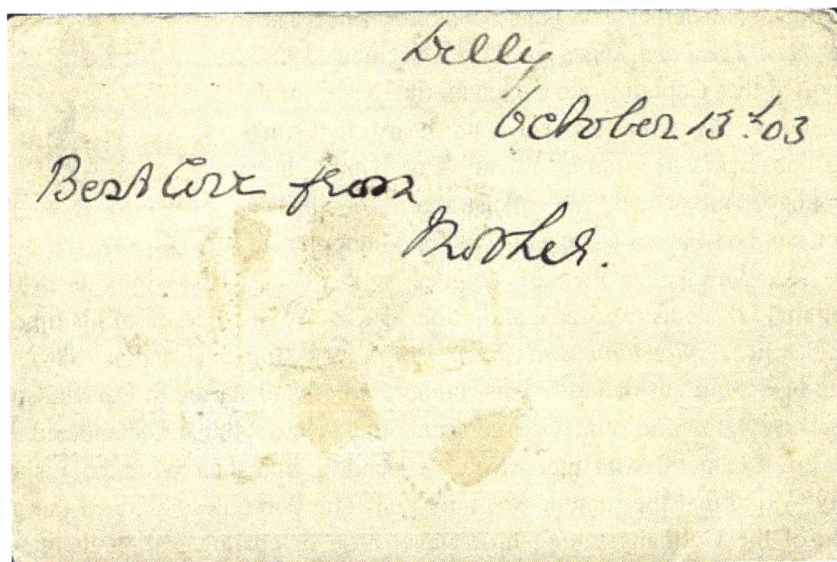

The postcard to Keith Tolhurst from Dili.

At that time East Timor was seen, both by the Portuguese and the Australians, as desperately poor. Wallace's description was still the most readily available one in both Britain and Australia – and it is worth noting that some of Creed's description does tally with that of Wallace. However Creed noted that there were 'large quantities of low grade ore which would pay well if near to existing smelting works' and, more significantly, 'the most important mineral resource will probably be 'petroleum' of which there is a natural spring, yielding several barrels of oil a day from a natural crevice in limestone country ... situated about eight miles from a harbour at an elevation of 2000 feet [which] will therefore be easy to convey from the wells to tank ships by an easily constructed pipeline.'[35] Creed then noted that a concession to extract the oil had already been obtained by a New South Wales Company, but gave no further details.

Creed's letter was forwarded to Joseph Chamberlain, Secretary of State for the Colonies, who asked for official clarification from the Portuguese whether the island was for sale. The *Northern Territory Times* on 23rd December 1904 reported that Captain John Strachan, the master of a trading vessel from Darwin, had heard that the Germans were negotiating to buy East Timor, but Strachan advocated an Australian purchase. Strachan had been a correspondent for Melbourne's *The Age* newspaper in New Guinea, and was described by the British Colonial Office as 'excitable and rather ignorant'. His account of his time in the Pacific, *Explorations and Adventures in New Guinea* (London 1888) had long been held in ridicule[36]. This rumour, which had started in Darwin, soon reached Melbourne, and George Reid, the Prime Minister, contacted the Governor-General who then wrote to London, and then wrote to Lisbon, only to find that the rumour was only that. The Portuguese claimed that the idea of the Germans setting up a naval base or coaling station there was somewhat far-fetched as there was only enough coal at Dili for the one Portuguese government ship based there.[37]

---

[35]    Patrick Freeman, a volunteer teacher at Baucau saw deposits of oil after a landslide near Dili in 1999, address to International Studies Teachers' Annual Meeting, Melbourne, 27th November 2000.

[36]    See H J Gibbney, 'John Strachan', *Australian Dictionary of Biography* Vol 6.

[37]    Most of the press coverage of East Timor and plans to sell it come from the article by Peter Hastings, *op.cit.*

However rumours of a possible German purchase continued. Part of this was probably connected with the growing fear of German naval shipping in the Pacific and Indian Ocean – only realised when the *Emden* was able to disrupt shipping lines in 1914. The next major rumour began when *The Age* in Melbourne on 14th October 1910 quoted an article in the *Tageliche Rundschau* (Berlin) which, when dealing with the deposing of the Portuguese King, noted that 'if Great Britain values a good understanding with Germany she can obtain it by giving effect to the Anglo-German Agreement of 1898 for the partition of the colonies of decayed Portugal'. The Federal Member for Capricornia, William Higgs mentioned in the Australian House of Representatives that there was an 'infamous suggestion of the Berlin newspaper ... to divide up the colonies which Portugal at present possesses' and that Australia should pay particular attention to what was happening and should also be consulted by the British as regards East Timor.

On 13th February 1912 the possible sale of East Timor was again raised in *The Age*. This time it quoted a Belgian journal, *Mouvement Geographique* saying that Germany was again interested in purchasing East Timor from Portugal, as well as the neighbouring island of Pulo Cambang. The columnist then noted that 'Germany is said to be greatly attracted in a scheme to compensate Portugal for the loss of these islands' and that 'Timor in hostile hands ... could effectively block Darwin and the Torres Strait traffic – more especially the future mail route from Darwin to Singapore to join the Malay and future Indian railway – and [East Timor] should [not] be handed over to Germany which has already most unnecessarily fortified its chief Papuan port, till it resembles a first class naval fortress'. The article ended with the note that the 'Portuguese Legation denied that there was any intent to sell or raise a loan upon the guarantees provided by those colonies'. Five years later, Professor Hans Meyer in an article entitled 'Germany and the Portuguese Colonies', published in *Deutsche Politik* on 18th May 1917, outlined some of the possibilities again.[38]

However the 'impending' 1912 negotiations with Germany were overshadowed by some more important developments in East Timor. *The Argus* on 19th February 1912 noted that Ramea tribesmen staged a rebellion

---

[38]    See 'Germany and the Portuguese Colonies', *The New Europe* (2 August 1917), pp. 88–91.

against the Portuguese and attacked Dili. Of the small number of Portuguese soldiers who were defending the town, two officers, Major Ingley and Lieutenant Silva were killed, along with some of their men. Government House was also looted in what became known as, in East Timorese folklore, the 'Great Rebellion'. *The Argus* noted that 'Port Dilly, the scene of the outrages, is closer to Port Darwin than Hobart is to Melbourne'. The already cash-strapped Portuguese government had to charter the *Zaire* for $$5,770 to transport 193 men from Mozambique to Timor in February 1912. These were able to defeat the rebels but the dissension quickly spread, and later another 100 men were sent to Timor.[39] When it became obvious that the situation in Timor was precarious, the Portuguese then sent even more soldiers from Portugal and Portuguese Africa – a special fund being raised to defray the costs. The Portuguese defeated the rebels – some 3,000 were said to have been killed in battle, and 4,000 captured.[40] A result of this rebellion was that the Portuguese decided to increase the level of their control over the island and African soldiers remained posted to Timor until the Second World War.[41] In 1914 the border disputes between the Dutch and the Portuguese were finally settled.

REPÚBLICA PORTUGUESA
2$50
Oficial de Infantaria 1903
TIMOR

During the First World War whilst The Netherlands remained neutral, Portugal did enter the war on the allied side in March 1916. Australia, nervous at the prospect of German merchant raiders (as in the case of the *Emden*), had a flotilla in the Timor Sea throughout 1915. In April 1915 an unnamed 'gentleman' from the University of Melbourne wrote to Andrew Fisher, the Prime Minister, suggesting that when the war had ended, Australia should try to acquire East Timor to create a 'hill station to lessen the strain of the long humid summer on the settlers of Northern Australia'. The suggestion was that as the Dutch and Portuguese were both losing money by holding West and East Timor, it would be relatively easy for Australia to step in. Fisher noted: 'I like the idea of possessing a summer resort for the settlers of Northern Australia and refer this matter to the Minister of External Affairs'. However, as with the previous schemes, nothing came of this plan. There was, however, another Australian proposal.

---

[39]    *The Times* 27 February 1912, p. 5; 20 April 1912, p. 5.
[40]    *The Argus* 26 August 1912.
[41]    Bernard Callinan, *op.cit.*, p. 19.

Uma rua de Loquiça — TIMOR.

On 12th December 1919 the British Consular Agent in Kupang in West Timor wrote that 'some two years ago an Australian Syndicate made a proposal to purchase Portuguese Timor for £3,000,000 but the venture has fallen through'. It was not long before the pre-war rumours of a sale to Germany gave war to the worry of the territory being bought by Japan.

## CHAPTER THREE

After the First World War, Australian contact with East Timor hinged on three issues: using the island as a stop-over for intercontinental flights to Australia, attempts to locate oil on the island or in nearby waters, and a concerted focus on trying to ensure that the Japanese did not get a foothold on the island. In some ways the three issues were separate, but in other ways they were all related.

With the emergence of air travel, several of the aviators of the period landed on the island of Timor. The aviation industry was given a jolt when the Australian government announced, in 1919, a prize of £10,000 for the first successful flight from Great Britain to Australia 'in a machine manned by Australians'. The air route between India and Timor had been the subject of a report by General Borton to the British Air Ministry in September 1919. The 500 miles from Timor to Darwin was regarded as the most hazardous part of the proposed route, and initially the Australian Defence Department offered to provide a 'sea watch'. Eventually when Ross (later Sir Ross) Smith made the journey in 1919, they used Atamboea in West Timor.[42] Most of the later aviators, as with the sailors of earlier years, chose Kupang rather than Dili as their base. James Bennett, Mrs Laures Bonney[43], (Sir) Alan Cobham[44] and (Sir) Charles Kingsford Smith all touched down on Timor – Sir                                                                      Ross

---

[42]    Nelson Eustis, *The Greatest Air Race: England – Australia 1919*, Adelaide: Rigby, 1994, passim.
[43]    Terry Gwynn-Jones. *Pioneer Airwoman: the story of Mrs Bonney*, Adelaide: Rigby, 1979, pp. 59–60.
[44]    Alan Cobham, *Australia and Back*, London: A&C Black, 1926, pp. 78–80.

Egreja matriz de Dilly. — TIMOR.

The church in Dili in the 1900s.

Hospital Timor Dilly

The Dili Hospital in the 1900s.

Smith was an exception using Baucau in East Timor on later flights. Obviously Portuguese aviators such as Major Sarmento Beires who flew from Macao in 1924 in an attempt to fly around the world, included East Timor in their itinerary.

Throughout the 1920s and 1930s rumours that the Portuguese were planning to sell or even lease East Timor to another power started again. As a result much energy in Australia and also in Britain was spent in dealing with these plans. There was a rumour of Portugal offering Timor to Japan in 1920. This seems to have originated from a report written by Major Edmund Leolin Piesse who had travelled around the region from September 1919 to March 1920 in order to assess Australia's role in the region.[45]

Piesse was born in Hobart and attended the Friends' School and then the Universities of Tasmania and Cambridge, graduating with a law degree in 1905. During the First World War he was Director of Military Intelligence and in 1918 was in the Prime Minister's Department as Director of the Pacific Branch. In 1919 he travelled extensively throughout the Far East and heard the rumour that Portugal had been planning to sell Macau to the Japanese. The Portuguese vigorously denied this, and there seems little likelihood of the comment being anything but a rumour. Piesse was to write many papers on Asian affairs including one on the future of East Timor which is held at the National Library of Australia. However in February 1921 Piesse wrote to the Department of External Affairs that 'Portuguese Timor is reported, on what seems to be good authority, to be under offer to Holland'. As with all the previous rumours, there was hurried communication with London and the Secretary-General of the Portuguese Foreign Ministry, Gonsalves Teixeira, was able to inform the British Minister in Lisbon that if the Portuguese government started parting with all its colonies in this fashion, it 'would be sufficient to provoke a revolution'. As it later turned out, it was the revolution in 1974 that was to lead to Portugal parting with her overseas provinces, not the other way round.

The Dutch government was also sounded out and the British Minister at The Hague, Sir Ronald Graham, reported to Lord Curzon, the British Foreign Secretary, that the Dutch Foreign Minister, Herman van Karnebeek, had said that:

---

45    Neville Meaney, 'E L Piesse and the problem of Japan', in Bridge, Carl & Attard, Bernard (eds). *Between Empire and Nation: Australia's External Relations from Federation to the Second World War*, Australian Scholarly Publishing: Melbourne 2000, pp. 73–92 at p. 83.

the question [of purchasing East Timor] had not been raised for some time past. About twenty years ago the idea had been mooted, and at that time the Netherlands Government would have liked to purchase Timor. At the present moment they were not in a financial position to entertain any such proposal, even if it had been made to them.

The Dutch Minister asked Sir Ronald Graham how the British government would react to the Dutch purchasing East Timor. Sir Ronald 'did not pursue the subject'.

The Australian government naturally was relieved when the rumours were proven to be ill-founded. Instead of a possible sale, the Portuguese decided to draw up plans to develop East Timor. They first wanted a telegraph transmitter in Dili to facilitate communications with Darwin. To try to monitor the situation a little more closely, plans were drawn up to establish a British consular office in Kupang, in West Timor – with the Australian government being asked to contribute to the cost. This did not eventuate.

However rumours of the possible sale of Timor started up again. On 13th August 1923 from Plymouth Pay, Lieutenant-Commander E F Jeffrey, Royal Naval Reserve, the purser on the RMS *Orsova* wrote to the Admiralty in London:

Recently in the Smoke Room of this ship I overheard a conversation, which was taking place between business men of standing; to the effect that the US Government have a scheme under weigh (sic) for the purchase of the Portuguese portion of Timor. I do not know whether this information is of any worth, but you are in a position to know, and so I have passed it on to you.

The letter was passed to the Foreign Office who noted:

We have heard rumours before that the Portuguese intended to sell Timor, but they have always been denied. Sir L Carnegie[46] has, I think more than once, made discreet enquiries on the subject in Lisbon. There are similar reports periodically regarding the Azores & other Portuguese 'relics of past glories'.

---

[46]    Sir Launcelot Carnegie, British Ambassador to Portugal 1924–28. Chris Cook, *Sources in British Political History 1900–1951*, Vol 2, records that none of Carnegie's papers survived.

Another hand then noted below:

> It is very unlikely that the Portuguese government will sell any of their past glories.

There is yet another story connected with the possible sale of East Timor to, in this case, a British businessman. It concerns William Kellie Smith, a Scottish eccentric who had made a fortune in rubber in Malaya. He was born in Scotland as 'William Smith' and had come to Malaya in 1889, aged 19. After gaining a concession to clear 360 hectares of land in Perak, he planted rubber trees and was also involved in tin mining. His Kinta Kellas Estate and Kinta Kellas Tin Dredging Company both made him a very large fortune, and William Kellie Smith, as he soon styled himself, returned to Scotland and married his sweetheart Agnes. They returned to Malaya and after the birth of their son Anthony, William Kellie Smith embarked on building a massive mansion for himself on his rubber estate near Batu Gajah, south of the important tin-mining city of Ipoh. The house was never completed as

Kellie's Castle, 2003.
Author's photograph

The English Cemetery, Lisbon.
Author's photograph

many of the workers succumbed to the 'Spanish influenza' which spread after the First World War, and Smith himself went to Portugal where he died of pneumonia at the Avenida Palace Hotel on 11th December 1926. He was buried in the English Cemetery in Lisbon on 13th December, and is listed in the church's burial register as a 'proprietor'. Many years later his unfinished house near Ipoh was opened to the public and is known as 'Kellie's Castle', being used for in some films.

There has been some speculation over the reason why William Kellie Smith went to Portugal, and the main reason cited in brochures available at Kellie's Castle was that he was negotiating with the Portuguese government for the purchase of East Timor. It is certainly possible that he might have been seeking to take out a lease on the island, but it seems unlikely that Smith, certainly a wealthy man, would have had the funds to purchase the whole island. It is possible, however, that he might have been planning to 'front' a syndicate for that purpose.

As mentioned earlier, there had been some Australian interest in the search for oil in East Timor before the First World War. Mr A T Trouton of Sydney had, as far back as 1909, obtained oil search concessions over three large areas of the eastern part of Portuguese Timor. Some initial drilling had resulted in the location of small oil reserves. In 1911 Arthur Staughton a pastoralist of Terang, in Victoria, bought out Trouton's interests.

Arthur John Staughton was the son of Samuel T Staughton, a long-time member of the Victorian Legislative Assembly. Born in 1876, Arthur Staughton went to Melbourne Grammar School 1887-94, serving in the 4th Light Horse during the First World War. A grazier at Keayang, near Terang, Victoria, he was Captain of the Camperdown Polo Team and represented Victoria in their polo competitions with South Australia. How Staughton became involved in the East Timor remains obscure but soon his company, the Timor Oil Company (and its subsidiary, Timor Oil Ltd) had begun a search for oil in East Timor, establishing a concession that would bear his name.

The Timor Petroleum Concessions Limited, formed with 15,000 shares of £1 each, had its registered offices in Sydney and the chairman of its board of directors was Dr James Elliott, still interested in the search for oil which he had seen about ten years earlier. The other directors were: Sir Joseph Carruthers, who had been Premier of New South Wales 1904-07; Sir James Graham MD, a prominent Sydney political campaigner and physician; Arthur Staughton; and Rutherford Affleck, a pastoralist from Minjah, Hawkesdale, Victoria[47].

Sir Joseph Carruthers consulted Professor Sir Edgeworth David, Professor of Geology at the University of Sydney and described as 'probably the most eminent geologist in the Southern Hemisphere'. The 1932 report for Timor Oil Limited notes:

Professor David was invited to accept an engagement to visit the locality and to report upon it, but he explained that the terms of his engagement as a University Professor precluded him from taking private engagements of this character. He recommended, however, that Mr H G Foxall BE, University of Sydney, should be deputed for the task. He said that Mr Foxall was, up to that time, one of the most, if not the most, promising student in geology who had passed through Sydney University.

---

[47] Rutherford Albert Affleck, born 1866, educated at Geelong Grammar School; pastoralist; of Glen Ronald, Glenthompson; purchased lease of Greenhills Station in 1894; and Minjah Station in 1898; died 1931.

Henry George Foxall was born in Sydney in 1884, the son of Edward and Margaret Foxall[48]. He went to Fort Street Model School and graduated with a Bachelor of Engineering from the University of Sydney in 1906.[49] His brother, John Stewart Foxall, born in Sydney in 1887, also studied engineering, graduating BE in 1913.[50] Henry Foxall worked with Professor Edgeworth David, and through him was offered a position with the Timor Petroleum Concessions Limited. On 1st September 1911, along with Staughton and Affleck, Foxall left Sydney on the E & A Company's ss *Empire* for Dili, arriving on 18th September. At Vessoro in East Timor, Foxall wrote a report:

Vessoro

November 4th, 1911

The Directors,

Timor Petroleum Concessions Ltd

Gentlemen,

I have the honour to submit herewith my report on the Petroleum Concessions held by your Company in the Island of Timor.

GENERAL.- The Concessions form part of an extensive oil field, which can be traced over the whole of the southern part of Portuguese Timor from Suai to Lau-Ten, and there is no doubt that it extends through the Dutch portion of the Island, and is an extension of the well-known oil-field comprising Sumatra, Java, and Borneo. The geological structure of the field consists of limestones, shales, and sandstones, which have been folded into a series of anticlines and synclines, the distance between successive folds being about two miles. The

---

[48] Edward William Foxall, an accountant, had married Margaret Nerissa Dobbie in 1881 at Ryde. In 1901 Edward Foxall contested the Federal Election for the NSW seat of Gwydir which was won by George Cruickshank. He died in 1926 at Woollahra.

[49] Henry Foxall married Eugenie M Hanley in 1912 at Wollongong. They had two daughters: Joan M, born in 1913 at Hunter's Hill, Sydney; and Sheila Margaret, born in 1916, also at Hunter's Hill (she married John Charles Harley Young in 1939 at Chatswood). Henry Foxall retired to Newport, New South Wales, and died on 22nd April 1966.

[50] John Foxall later worked as head surveyor for Sons of Gwalia mine in Western Australia until the First World War when he served in the Tunnelling Corps. He returned to Western Australia where he worked until his death on 12th March 1967. He was buried in the Karrakatta Cemetery, Perth.

axes of the folds lie in a north-easterly and south-westerly direction, and it is on the tops of the anticlines that the petroleum deposits must be sought.

The oil is contained in the sandstones above referred to, of which I have identified three distinct horizons:-

1. The Atalele horizon, exposed on the Atalele Concessions and at Bualiu.
2. The Mete-Hou horizon, at Mete-Hou and Iribin.
3. The Bibiluto horizon, exposed at Bibiluto, some 20 miles west of Vessoro.

There is no indication, and indeed it is highly improbable, that these are the only oil-bearing horizons on the field, but I have not been able to positively identify any others.

(1) ATALELE HORIZON – The geological features of this horizon are not very distinct owing to the fact that the outcrops in the immediate neighbourhood are obscured by cultivation and by debris resulting from land slips, and for definite information it will be necessary to rely to a great degree on the results of boreholes. So far as can be seen from the data available, the sandstones lie between beds of shale on the lower side and limestone, above, and are fairly soft and medium grained in texture, and of a suitable nature for carrying oil.

(2) METE-HOU HORIZON – This is the horizon which is the best defined of the three and good sections are available in which to study it. It consists, where exposed, of soft, compact, medium-grained sandstones of a greenish tint, and is about 200-ft thick. The overlying and underlying strata are respectively greenish-grey shales and hard, compact limestone, the limestone being succeeded at a depth of about 80-ft by shales. The distance between this horizon and No 1 is probably about 700-ft. There is ample evidence from the indications mentioned hereunder that these sandstones carry a large quantity of petroleum, and if tapped at a sufficient depth to ensure freedom from impoverishment due to oxidation and leakage, they should be able to be profitably worked.

(3) BIBILUTO HORIZON – My attention was attracted to this horizon by the report of the existence of a mud volcano in the district. As mud volcanoes are characteristic of oil-bearing country all over the world, and particularly in the other East Indian fields; I visited the locality and found an exposure of very soft, porous, and friable sandstones, whose thickness I was not able to define. These sandstones are, to my mind, of an ideal nature for the accumulation of petroleum, and also for the recovery of the same, since their porous nature will not only facilitate the storage of large quantities of petroleum. but also will offer very little resistance to the percolation of the oil to the bore-holes.

Unfortunately, as the country surrounding was flat, alluvial plain, I could gather very little information as to the depth of this horizon below that of Mete-Hou, but a rough computation shows it to be from 300-ft to 500-ft.

THE CONCESSIONS – The Concessions at present held by the Company are seven in number, and are shown on the accompanying plan 'A'. They will be hereafter referred to as:

1. Mete-Hou Concession.
2. Mete-Hou Concession No 2 (applied for by Mr Staughton as No 4).
3. Atalele Concession.
4. Ira-Muni Concession.
5. Iribin Concession No 1 (applied for as No 1).
6. Iribin Concession No 2 (applied for as No 2).
7. Bualiu Concession (applied for as No 3).

METE-HOU CONCESSIONS, Nos 1 and 2 (See Plan 'B') – The total area of these Concessions is approximately 375 acres (150 hectares). They are situated partly on the side of a steep mountain about 1000-ft high, and partly on the top of the same mountain. The sandstone horizon above referred to as the Mete-Hou horizon outcrops approximately as shown on the plan and all the evidence tends to show that although, naturally, where the strata are exposed they have become impoverished by oxidation and leakage, if tapped at a sufficient distance from the exposure, say, at a depth of 250-ft to 300-ft, there would be a large supply of oil available. The indications referred to have been described in previous reports and I recapitulate them briefly here.

1. A strong oil seep from the rocks exposed at low tide on the shore. There is no difficulty in getting a bottle full of oil at any time, and I found that by putting down a charge of dynamite quite a strong flow of oil could be obtained locally for a short time, while for twenty yards round oil could be seen issuing from every crack in the rocks. Shown at 'A' on plan.

2. A continuous supply of burning gas issuing from the ground at 'B'.

3. The oil was tapped by a hole sunk 31-ft ('C' on plan). The oil maintains a constant level in the hole, and cannot be lowered by bailing with a tin on the end of a rope. It has been reported that the further sinking of this hole was prevented by, an inrush of sea water, but the water now in the hole is quite fresh even at high tide.

4. The oil was again tapped at a depth of nearly 300-ft (150-ft below sea level) at 'D'. On listening at the mouth of the pipe, gas can be heard bubbling from below, and it can be ignited at the surface.

5. A second indication of gas not hitherto described has been found at 'E'. It consists of a tract of clayey material which, when broken fresh, has a distinct smell of petroleum.

The top of the anticline cuts across the south-eastern corner of the original concession, as shown by the double line, and the area giving a maximum yield of petroleum will be found lying within a distance of about 30 chains on each side of this line, although the ground outside this limit must also be tried. Reference to the plan will show that a large proportion of the area originally including the Mete-Hou sandstone will be unproductive so far 'as that horizon is concerned, as it has either been removed by erosion or impoverished by exposure. This area, however, will be fully productive as regards the lower horizons of oil. I had a bore-hole started near the top of the anticline below the sandstone to prospect the lower strata, but at the time of writing no oil has been met to a depth of 185 ft or 130ft below sea level.

ATALELE AND IRA-MUNI CONCESSIONS – Very little definite information could be gained about these concessions, as the geological structure was obscured by secondary deposits resulting from land slips and erosion. The surface indications are:-
1. A flow of gas about the centre of the Atalele Concession. When I first saw this it was not burning, but on the application of a match to the fissures in the ground the gas at once ignited.
2. An oil seep in the middle of a rice field in the Ira-Muni Concession. This oil has been described as 'asphalt-like', but is quite fluid although heavier than the oil found at Vessoro, the asphalt-like appearance being due to its admixture with the soil where it flows out.
    The most salient geological feature of these concessions is a large outcrop of igneous rock, which has been intruded into the oil-bearing strata at the top of the anticline, as shown on the plan. These rocks are, of course, barren of oil themselves, and will also have impoverished the strata through which they have burst by volatilising the oil contained therein. The thick nature of the oil at Ira-Muni is probably due to partial volatilisation in this manner. It will readily be seen, then, that the most productive parts of these concessions are rendered valueless, and I would strongly recommend that further areas be taken up here as shown on the plan by dotted lines. These areas will be very slightly, if at all, productive in the Atalele horizon, but fully productive in the Mete-Hou and Bibiluto horizons.

IRIBIN AND BUALIU CONCESSIONS – In these concessions there is an extensive exposure of the sandstone of the Mete-Hou horizon, with numerous indications of petroleum in the shape of gas flows, none of which, however, are to be compared with that at Mete-Hou. These sandstones will be greatly impoverished by oxidation and exposure, and the value of the concessions will depend almost entirely on the production from lower horizons. Since, however, as mentioned above, these horizons give every indication of being highly valuable, I have no hesitation in saying that these concessions are of very considerable importance, especially in view of the fact that the natural configuration of the surface renders it particularly suitable for the erection of refining works, etc, and the water supply available is apparently inexhaustible.

The direction of the anticlinal axis is here assumed to be parallel to that at Mete-Hou. but it is possible. Judging from the disposition of the gas flows, that it has a trend more to the east and west. For this reason the Bualiu Concession has been retained, although, from the plan 'A' the profitable working area seems very small. The direction of the axis will be proved by boring on the Iribin Concessions, and then that at Bualiu can be retained or forfeited as thought best. In this concession the horizon exposed, as shown on the plan, is the Atalele horizon, and therefore the Mete-Hou horizon is unexposed and the yield therefrom will be full.

SUMMARY – To sum up, there is every indication that this field will prove as important as the other East Indian fields. The geological structure and the indications are similar in each case, and the geographical position of the island indicates that this is an extension of the neighbouring productive fields. The concessions are all situated in favourable positions on the tops of anticlines, with the possible exception of that of Bualiu. Commercial results are to be looked for in every case, excepting perhaps, in part, in the Mete-Hou Concessions, from deep-boring to tap the unexposed horizons, particularly that at Bibiluto, which I consider the most important of the three described. For this purpose I would recommend that a plant be secured with the capacity of at least 2,000-ft and that the earlier wells at least be sunk to the full depth of the oil-bearing beds, irrespective of any oil found on the way, careful and minute records being kept in order to obtain the fullest knowledge possible of the available stores of oil.

The most favourable areas for boring are indicated on the plans by double dotted lines; but in this, of course, the management will be guided in every case by the results of work already done.

(Signed) H. G. FOXALL,

(B.E. Univ. Sydney).

[Note: The plans made by Mr Foxall accompany this report.]

To this, Arthur Staughton added:

Sydney.

December 1st, 1911

The Board of Directors,

Timor Petroleum Concessions Ltd,

Sydney.

Gentlemen,

I have to report that we arrived at Dilly, 9.30 pm on Friday, September 18th, when Bryant[51] and I went off in the first available boat to see what arrangements, if any, were made or to be made, for receiving our men and cargo at that late hour. On reaching the shore, which was about half a mile row from the *Empire*, we found Dr Lobo awaiting us, and on presenting him with all necessary papers etc, he consented straight away to act for the new Company, as agent in Dilly, and I might mention that both he and his son Peter have given most invaluable assistance and gone considerably out of their way to further our interests, and certainly without their aid it would have been impossible for us to have fixed up everything to get away from Dilly inside at least a fortnight.

---

[51] G H Bryant, local representative of Timor Oil Limited in East Timor. His copy of the prospectus: *Petroleum Oil: the history of oil exploration in the island of Timor, prepared from the records of various companies in New South Wales (Australia); together with several experts' reports made in connection therewith,* Sydney: Timor Oil Ltd, 1932, is held at the University of Melbourne library. It gives Bryant's address as '28 Gordon St, W Coburg, Melbourne', and Bryant is listed at this address in the 1930 Sands and Mcdougalls Directory of Melbourne. There is a George Henry Bryant who died on 19th October 1947 at Parkville, Melbourne, aged 76, and was buried two days later at the Coburg Cemetery (CofE A section, no 246). He is listed in the newspaper death notice as 'late of South Morang', and there is no gravestone. There is also George Henry Bryant who died in June 1961 in Melbourne, aged 78, and was buried at the Fawkner Cemetery (GR2A 6/12/151) alongside his wife Mabel who died six years earlier; and this is possibly the man who worked in Timor.

Engaging prows, we had our cargo landed about 12 pm, and put into the Customs House Saturday morning. The Governor [Manuel de Abreu Ferreira de Carvalho] being absent, we interviewed the Chief Secretary, and after a lot of persuading on our part, we successfully chartered the gunboat, *The Dilly*, to take us as far as Baucow, 60 miles on our road, on the following Monday morning, leaving at 5 am.

Having completed these arrangements, it taking well on to nightfall, it was necessary to clear our eight tons of stuff through the Customs on Sunday, and have it transhipped on board *The Dilly* that day, which was satisfactorily done, so we were able to leave the town in time, all on board with the exception of our recently engaged cook, who missed the boat. The captain absolutely refusing to wait one minute for him, we sailed for Baucow, arriving there the same afternoon, the 18th September.

As there is no harbour or pier at this important station, it was necessary to again unload into surf boats, and have the whole of our stuff again transhipped from these boats and carried the last hundred yards on the heads of natives through the surf.

Baucow being about 900-ft above the sea, we rode up, and were met by the Commandant, who was most obliging and put the Government House at our disposal. Wanting to push on, and having only some 200 carriers present, we decided to leave the next day with what they could take, so on the 19th we left Baucow and arrived that night at Fatumaca. Left Fatumaca, which is a native village, at 6 o'clock, and after crossing a range of mountains 3,500-ft in height, arrived at Ossui same evening, engaged carriers, sent one lot back to Baucow and another lot on to Vessoro with the stores as they arrived.

Leaving Ossui 7 o'clock, we arrived at our destination at 2.30 pm September 21st. Inspecting the station, we were most favourably impressed with the way it has been maintained by Barros under his charge.

The huts are as follows: three living huts, of four rooms each; one dining-room, with pantry attached; one kitchen and cook's room; one bathroom, with water laid on; one store-room, detached; and three huts for natives; the whole being artistically laid out with garden and pebble paths just above high tide on the sea shore.

The next morning we inspected the Mete-Hou Concession. This inspection showed us that the different reports already received with regard to surface indications were in the main correct, and after carefully inspecting the bore where the plant was stationed, we decided it was quite impracticable to go on with this, as not only was the casing stuck, but the pump and some 130-ft of broken rope were down the hole, and to extract same was out of the question, so we immediately set about to decide on a new site, leaving Warren and his two men with a gang of 25 natives to dismantle machinery and overhaul same with a view to transportation.

The geologist (Mr Foxall) having fixed definitely on a locality some 13 chains east and nearer the sea shore and about 60-ft above sea level, we all set to work to clear a space of about two chains square of all timber and undergrowth, to enable us to set up the plant. The transportation was even for this short distance, a most tedious job, and took us six days before we got to work boring, as all the heavy parts-boiler, engine, etc had to be let down and pulled up the hills with block and tackle. In the meantime, having had three natives on at sinking a well, we were able, on the 30th September, to start boring in the bottom of the well, now sunk 17 ft.

Having everything now going satisfactorily, we – Mr Foxall, Mr Affleck and myself – decided to inspect the adjoining country, and we were fortunate enough to discover on the side of the mountain east of Vessoro, only about 1½ chains from our boundary, another place which smelt strongly of petroleum, and had recently been also on fire, for a space of 10 yards square. On returning to camp, I immediately wrote Dr Lobo asking him to secure this concession for our Company, without lapse of time, and also to inform us what area we are entitled to take up. His reply to same was to the effect that if we put up a post with the name of the Company on it at each corner, was all that was necessary in the meantime.

Not being able to find any other indications of oil in this locality, we then decided to inspect the Atalele Concessions, where we shifted camp on the 4th October. Atalele being about four miles due north of Vessoro, but after following in the bed of a dry river and winding round the mountains, we arrived at our camping ground, about 10 chains off the concession, after five hours' riding.

We also found here, as in Vessoro, that all indications and surface shows were practically true to reports, with the exception that the gas on Atalele was not on fire. On holding a match over the place it caught fire and exploded with a bang, and we left it blazing away. We think, it absolutely essential, after carefully following the boundaries of these two blocks, that it is undoubtedly to the interests of the company that we should secure more ground adjoining these concessions, either for working them ourselves or for the purpose of sale.

On completing a thorough inspection of these concessions, we decided to split up and return to camp by different routes, and I found, by going via Tualo, that it was practically a good road all the way, with the exception of a few steep pinches in it, which is quite natural, as Atalele is 1,200 ft above this place; but the greater portion of road a coach and four could be driven up it in its present state, and it would be quite feasible to get what machinery was required to work these concessions via this route.

On returning home and hearing from one of the workmen (a native who lives about 16 miles north-east of here) that there was also a smell near where he lived similar to that at Vessoro, we thought it worth investigating, so immediately set out at 5 am, returning at 8 pm, after a most satisfactory day.

On finding the locality, it was quite impossible not to notice the strong smell of gas, and on holding a match down it also lit up with a roar and a bang, and in fact, I think there is a greater escape of gas here than any of the other places we have seen, with the exception of the big fire at Mete-Hou, and I might mention that it looked, to my lay mind, that it would probably be the most extensive oil field of any of the localities we have inspected so far.

On returning home, as before mentioned, I immediately sent a messenger away to the Local Commandant at Tualo to engage carriers to enable us to shift camp to the new field, so that we could give it a thorough inspection, living on the ground. Again, as usual, getting away before daylight, we arrived at our destination, and after picking a site for a camp and giving our ponies an hour's feed, we all split up and rode away in different directions, to enable us to get a lay of the country, and if possible to procure some sort of game for food for us and our men. On getting back to our proposed camp at dark we were pleased to see our carriers just coming in.

Up before daylight, we were not long in coming to some of the following conclusions:-

The position of this find is situated about three miles east of Tualo, some ten miles from Vessoro, and as it is practically level all the way, with a little expense, a motor-car could run from one concession to the other.

The name of the kingdom is Iribin, so in future these concessions will be referred to by that name. They are situated practically in a basin, with the hills on three sides and the sea on the other. The formation of the country is much the same for about two miles square – all undulating country, the highest point being in the centre known as 'Kohoda', a native village, which is 450 ft above sea level.

There is a valley right round this hill, and one large river on each side; in fact, one of the rivers is a long way the largest we have seen on the whole island, having a breadth of fully 80 to 90 yards of swiftly running water, with a depth of up to 2 ft, 6 in, after five months' drought. The other river stops running before it reaches the sea, mainly because it is not anything like so large, and also on account of its having a great quantity of the water converted into irrigation channels higher up for the purpose of watering very extensive rice fields, which are all included in the concessions secured. One of these fields is quite 40 to 60 acres in extent, and only some 150 ft above sea level, and being situated on the opposite side of the hill Kohoda, before mentioned, to the sea. It will give some indication of the lay of the country when I mention that fully one-half of this valuable concession is no higher than 170 ft above sea level, which means that it will require the expenditure of hardly any money in making roads, etc, to fully prospect this show.

After spending three days carefully inspecting the surrounding country, we were unable to hear of or find any other surface indications. The two previous nights, when lying on our stretchers, we could not help noticing a very bright fire burning with more than usual brilliancy on the side of the hill about 600 yards away. After looking up for the cause of it in daylight, and not being able to locate anything from our camp, I decided to ride up and personally investigate. On hunting round for some time, I found, in the middle of a maize cultivation, a similar indication of extinct gas as we found at Vessoro. Getting a couple of natives, we immediately set them to work with sticks to dig a hole, and, after getting down about 18 in. I held a match down to the hole, and, as we expected, it immediately lit up, which, of course, explained our nightly fire; and, getting hold of the local chief, he confessed that it was lit every night to do the cooking, etc, and then extinguished with dry dirt in the morning, so we should not find it.

After this discovery it naturally gave us a fresh impetus to look further afield. Although the natives one and all assuring us that there were not other indications of gas or mineral anywhere else in the district, not being satisfied, Mr Affleck and I decided to travel east into the adjoining country across the River Irraberri, which is the name of the big one before mentioned. We put in the greater part of the day without any indications whatever, strangely meeting on the top of a 500 ft hill densely covered with bamboos etc, about 5 o'clock in the afternoon. Having decided to examine the opposite side of the hill, we again separated, he taking one face and I the other. I had only proceeded about half a mile when, wounding a deer, which ran past me, crawling after him on my hands and knees through some bamboos along a deer track, I was greatly surprised to see in the centre of one of the thickets with a track right through it, the ground all disturbed in places with limestone boulders on the surface, and something similar to our other fields, covering an area of nearly a chain long by half wide. On coming closer I immediately saw that the far side was well alight, some of the fire in places covering up two to three feet from down in the cracks. Of course, I immediately put up a peg with my name and date of discovery, as we did on the previous finds, which I ascertained was sufficient to conserve all rights for our Company and prevent any other person jumping these claims.

Getting back to the camp as soon as possible I immediately sent off a messenger to the Commandant, informing him what we had found and asking him to come and verify same, which he did next morning. Not being able to find any other indications in the surrounding district, we then decided to put up our boundary pegs, and after carefully going into the matter, decided to cut up this indicated mineral bearing area into three separate concessions, this being decided on for certain reasons that would take too long to enumerate. The descriptions of the boundaries are as follows:-

IRIBIN CONCESSION No 1 – Commencing at the intersection of the west bank of the Lubatura River with the sea coast, and bounded thence on the west by straight lines passing in a northerly direction, to the village of Nunoa, and thence to the village of Hiauli. Then again on the north in a straight line passing in an easterly direction to the village of Haibubu thence on the east by straight lines passing to the village of Kohoda, and thence due south to the sea coast; thence again on the south by that coast westerly till the point of commencement.

IRIBIN CONCESSION No 2 – Commencing on the south-eastern corner of No 1 Concession just described, and thence on the west by the eastern boundary of that concession to the village of Haibubu aforesaid.

Thence on the north by a line passing due east of the western bank of the River Irriberri. Thence on the east by that bank of that river southerly till its intersection with the sea, thence on the south by the sea coast westerly to the point of commencement.

BUALUI CONCESSION No 3 – Commencing at the intersection of the eastern bank of the River Irriberri and the sea coast, thence on the south by that sea coast, bearing generally north-east to the western bank of the River Ueaei about 1,760 metres. Thence on the east by a line bearing due north 1,150 metres, thence on the north by a line bearing due west to the eastern bank of the River Irriberri aforesaid, thence on the west by that bank of that river southerly till the point of commencement.

Having defined these boundaries and the preliminary necessary stages of the act being complied with in the way of pegging each corner, and word having been sent to us that the Governor and party were shortly to be expected to pay us a visit at Vessoro, we packed up camp and returned home. Having some time at our disposal, we then decided to make out and peg the boundaries of the land already applied for adjoining Mete-Hou, which will be known as Mete-Hou No 2, Further Concessions. The pegged boundaries are as follows:-

Commencing at the south-east corner of Mete-Hou Concession and bounded thence on the south by the sea coast to a point 1 kilometre east of that corner. Thence on the east by a straight line bearing due north half a kilometre. Thence on the north by a straight line passing due west to the eastern boundary of the Mete-Hou Concession, and thence on the west by that boundary of that concession southerly till the point of commencement.

On the Governor arriving at Vessoro with six of his administrators, he first informed us that he intended to push on to Tualo the some night, and after having breakfasted at 11 o'clock we started to show him around our works, etc, and I am pleased to say that it took very little persuading on our part to induce him to stay on with us that night, it not being till late the next evening, after thoroughly inspecting all our shows etc, that he was able to leave.

I might mention that this was the first time he had ever been on our side of the Island, and having previously visited all the other oil concessions, he was most favourably impressed with what we had to show him in the way of surface shows, and more especially with the work done and being done at present.

He informed us that we had far more to show, both as regards indications of oil and more to show in development works than the other companies, even after knowing that the Pualaca Company had expended something like £15,000 already.

(Mr Staughton's report here contains a series of questions put to the Governor, and the replies thereto, relating to the laws of the Portuguese Timor Colonial Government, concerning the Company's position as holders of mining leases or prospecting licenses, and particularly in regard to what rights, privileges, and obligations would attach to the Company's holdings. The replies were very full and sympathetic, and the questions and replies are in the possession of the Company and will be produced to any person or company bona-fide treating for the property.)

Everything now being in a shipshape condition at Vessoro, with all our new concessions secured, and the boring at the new hole going on as well as could be expected, the bore being down some 130 ft, we were therefore left without a job, so Mr Affleck and self decided that it might be to the interests of our Company in the future to have an authentic report of the other leading English petroleum company. We left Vessoro on the 26th October, and journeyed west, getting to Viquique that night. Knowing that there was what was called a mud volcano at Bibiluto, some three hours' ride. we left early in the morning to see this show, and I may mention, were not at all favourably impressed. Leaving Viquique the next morning we only got as far as a native village, about two hours from Luca. On arriving there the next day and not being able to procure carriers, it was necessary to stay over the following night. From here we rode to Locluta, the whole day travelling in the bed of a dry river. it being most distressingly hot for our carriers and ponies, arriving there very late in the evening. From Locluta we rode to Crebis, staying there that night. Getting an early start we arrived at Pualaca for breakfast after six hours' riding. Being most hospitably entertained by Mr Green, the Manager, who also kindly allowed us to make a thorough inspection of their whole concession, either accompanying us himself or sending his expert driller (Mr McKeown) with us, and both of these gentlemen spared neither time nor trouble in answering all our numerous questions in a straightforward manner, giving us a lot of valuable information, which they were in a position to do, considering they both had spent some 16 years petroleum mining in Borneo and Sumatra with the Royal Dutch Company.

I do not intend to give a detailed account of what we saw, as I am not writing a report on Pualaca, but will mention that they have thoroughly prospected this concession only to a shallow depth, under the supervision of Dr Webber, one of the most able oil experts of the world, who has been continuously on the ground for 17 months, directing all operations, and who undoubtedly has implicit faith in the ultimate success of their field.

Leaving here after lunch on the third day, we started on our return journey to Dilly. Our ponies knocking up, it was not till two o'clock next morning that we arrived back at Crevis, having to walk the greater portion of the way over a range of mountains 4,500-ft. high. Our baggage not coming to hand, we decided, after a couple of hours' rest, to push on. Getting a change of ponies, we arrived at Laclo at 2.30 that afternoon, getting our first meal since leaving Pulaca. Again getting fresh ponies, we left after an hour's spell for Mintanaro, where we found a rest house provided by the Government, and it now being 1.30 a.m, we thought it advisable to camp, instead of making Era, which was our intention. After a short stay we again got on the road, and passing through Era, about an hour and a half's ride, we reached Dilly for breakfast (which Dr Lobo was kind enough to provide), after crossing another range of 1500-ft. height.

Getting practically all the necessary legal work in train, and having a week at our disposal, we decided to further inspect the Western portion of the

Island of Portuguese Timor; so leaving Dilly after two days, at 4 p.m, we rode via Tebar, reaching Liquico at 9 p.m, where we were hospitably entertained by the Commandant, who is second in command on the Island. Getting fresh ponies, and the moon now being up, we rode on with Signor Rocha Carvalho, who kindly asked us to stay the night at his plantation, called Tahata, 2,400-ft, above sea level. From Tahata we travelled to Fatu Bessi, via Gleno and Tebar, back to Dilly, which we reached on the 16th November.

Before concluding, I would like to mention that I have been most careful to only mention facts, and not in any way to include in my report anything with regard to the geological consideration, etc, of any of the fields inspected, as Mr Foxall has thoroughly dealt with this matter, and, I feel sure, can do so in a much more able manner; but before closing, would like to mention that, personally, I am more than satisfied with what I have seen. Undoubtedly the surface shows are more than can be desired. Talking to numerous oil experts here, they all assure me that they have never seen, or even heard of, such good indications, on the surface, of oil in very large quantities at a greater depth, anywhere else in the world, which, of course, I cannot vouch for, but will conclude by saying that I am quite satisfied to put my own money into prospecting at a great depth, and if the present Company do not want or require these new concessions, taken up in my name for them, will have great pleasure in developing this field in conjunction with Mr Affleck, who is solely of the same opinion, at our own expense.

(Signed) A J Staughton

Soon afterwards Alfred Warren, who had been in East Timor for a few years, added:

Sydney
1st February 1912

The Chairman of Directors,
Timor Petroleum Concessions Ltd,
Sydney.

Dear Sir,

I beg to report my return to Sydney per s.s. *Empire* this 1st February and now hand you particulars of the work conducted at the Concessions by myself and staff since arriving there in September last.

After arriving at Vessoro, the plant was removed from the old site to one chosen by Mr Foxall. After a lot of trouble in keeping the casing following the bore as we travelled, we got down to 308 feet. We then found it impossible to go any further, as the plant was too light to deal with the difficult country, and to be successful, much heavier plant with special drills adapted for deep well-boring will be required, as well as larger casing, in addition to that now on the Concessions.

Mr Staughton left Vessoro on the 25th October, and before his departure, instructed me to go down as far as I could with this particular bore, and, if unsuccessful in obtaining oil, to sink a shaft on the site chosen near the living quarters. These instructions were carried out, and we discovered a seepage of oil at 27 feet; I then sank a further 4 or 5 feet through the sand, but the oil apparently did not increase.

On completing this well I commenced to remove the plant to it, but then found that there would be insufficient time to do any boring, as I was instructed by Mr Staughton to return by the s.s. *Empire* leaving in January.

I then decided to erect a store-house, which was done, and all tools, gear, etc, safely stored, and before leaving Vessoro on January 3rd to travel overland to Dilly, everything was made secure. I left a caretaker in charge of the Company's property, but, in consequence of an insurrection by the natives against the Portuguese at different points on the Island, I was obliged to engage 4 native soldiers to assist him, otherwise the Company's property would have been left unprotected. I have every reason to believe that, on returning to the Island, everything will be found intact.

I have been going to the Island now for the past three years, and there is at the present time a bigger seepage of oil and a larger escape of gas on various portions of the Company's Concessions than at any previous time within my knowledge. I cannot account for this, but as far as it is possible to form an opinion, there appears to be every indication of tremendous oil deposits on the Island. but before any operations could be carried out effectively, it will be necessary to purchase a heavier plant, capable of getting down to at least 2,000 feet.

My engagement with the Company having now ceased, I will be pleased to afford my services if required in any further operations that may be decided upon.

Yours faithfully,
(Signed) Alfred Warren

Quoting more of the 1932 report for Timor Oil Limited:

It may here be stated that we had a field manager, Mr W D Stevenson, and a staff working at the Concessions up to February 1913, but Stevenson and his staff unexpectedly returned to Sydney on the 24th February of that year.

A change of managers was necessary on account of the termination of Mr Stevenson's engagement. Negotiations were completed by cable with Mr W J McKeown, a borer from Sumatra, who should have arrived in Timor on the 9th July 1913, but, for unexplained reasons, he advised the Company to await his arrival until after the next rainy season. That meant a loss of work which might have been done in 1913.

Stevenson reported to the directors of Timor Petroleum Concessions, Ltd, that, on arriving at the Concessions in February 1913, he found everything as was represented to him by the Company in Sydney. All the surface indications were very prominent and the oil was noticeable on the beach, and in places was seen to be percolating through the rocks. Everything he saw tended to confirm the reports of Mr Staughton and others.

He carried out certain works of an essential character regarding the store-room, the clearing of about three acres of heavy scrub and bush surrounding the headquarters. Sickness intervened amongst the Europeans, and he had to send back two or three of his staff to Dilly.

Other work done consisted of the construction of a grade 100 ft x 60 ft. This was to provide a foundation for the rig, and a casing cellar 20 ft deep cribbed up with poles, and with necessary cuts and ditches, was also put down. A store was also built for the housing of the derrick lumber, cables, etc. A bamboo water line was also put in to take the water from the springs at the top of the mountain to a reservoir on the site for storing the water, which was to be used for all purposes for which water would be required.

Mr Stevenson then stated that he had other troubles to contend with, some of his staff, and himself, becoming ill off and on until the time of his departure. For that reason he thought it advisable to return to Sydney with his staff rather than stay on through the wet season, with a broken-down staff unfit to do the work.

Other than the above improvements, very little value came to the Company from Stevenson's work.

In 1914, the new field manager, Mr McKeown, arrived on the concessions, erected a boring rig, and commenced operations.

Mr McKeown was a man specially recommended as having had experience with the Eastern Oil Companies in Sumatra and Borneo. He was strongly recommended on account of his capacity and his experience in oil drilling. He also knew something of the geological side of oil exploration.

A new plant had been sent down from Sydney, of an American type, obtained from Overall McCray Limited. This plant, it was stated, was probably the best that, up to that time, had ever been assembled in the Southern Hemisphere, having a capacity for boring to a depth of 3,000 feet. The Company was never able, with its old plant, to test the ground to a greater depth than 280 feet, and at that depth oil and gas indications were present, when boring had perforce to cease owing to the incapacity of the plant. The advice of the experts, who, from time to time, had been consulted, was to the effect that the oil strata should be found at a depth of from 700 to 1,000 feet, the average depth in the fields of the adjacent islands, Sumatra and Borneo.

In November 1914, Mr McKeown's report showed that boring was then proceeding satisfactorily, and that a depth of 270 feet had been reached. At 70 feet some oil of a heavy nature was met with, and at 165 feet gas was struck, and the latter being an oil indication. Mr McKeown, in the light of his experience in other parts of the Malay Archipelago, expressed the hope that oil would not be struck at a less depth than 800 feet, as at that depth or a greater depth the oil was more likely to be permanent than if found in a shallower strata.

At 270 feet some difficulty was experienced in continuing the bore, and until some additional parts and heavier tools and casing arrived at the concessions there was a little delay in carrying it to a greater depth. About this time the Great War broke out, just when the Company was expecting the bore to reach the main oil-bearing bed. A fair gusher had been struck at 320 feet.

This gusher caused the oil and the gas to throw up the tools with the oil into the air over the top of the derrick, and on to an acre or so of surrounding land.

Instructions had been sent to Mr McKeown, which he faithfully carried out, to cut off the water where the gusher had occurred at 320 feet, so as not to interfere with the supply of oil which had been tapped at that depth. He was instructed then to proceed further until he got down to the zone (which he reckoned to be 700 feet deep) of the major supply.

Boring proceeded until we got into the limestone formation, which, so we were informed by Mr McKeown, was taken to be the indication in Borneo and Sumatra that we were in the final overhead strata before getting on the oil reservoir below.

We were fully expecting, in 1914, just prior to the war, to be advised that the bore had cut through the remaining few feet which, we were told, was all that was in the way of reaching to the main oil supply.

Unfortunately, just at this time, the bearing rod broke off at the part connecting up with the actual brace and bit. It was found also, when attempts were being made to fish the broken parts out, after the main rod had been withdrawn, that the boring tool itself had been damaged. Evidently some nuts or bolts had got loose, with the result that the bore was working and grinding out a core an inch or so wider than the core above it. This put a ledge in the place where the tubing should be, causing a cavity of about an inch wider than that above it, and in attempting to fish out the broken parts, this ledge absolutely restricted the possibility of successfully withdrawing these broken fragments.

The Company was advised by cable and otherwise, and was informed that it was necessary to get a special tool to grind out the brace and bit and other broken parts. Messrs Overall McCray Ltd. were consulted, and they stated that they had the necessary tool to do the work. The cost would have been only a few pounds. The Company was preparing to buy this and send it down, when they were confronted with the fact that, owing to the war, all shipping had ceased between Australia and Portuguese Timor. It was found that it would be necessary to charter a special vessel, at a cost of something like £2,000, to carry a tool that would cost not more than £20 at the most. It became manifest to the directors that, with the continuance of the War, and with the cessation of direct shipping communication, it was impossible to carry on the work and to keep up the staff at the concessions.

Mr McKeown was, therefore, directed to cease work, and his engagement was temporarily suspended until such period when it might be resumed with fair chances of success once peace was restored.

Moreover, at an earlier stage, it was apparent to the directors of the Company that the capital available for a resumption of work later on was quite inadequate. This view was submitted to the shareholders of the then existing Company (Timor Petroleum Concessions Limited), and they concurred in a proposal for the formation of a reconstructed company to be called Timor Oil Limited. It was not contemplated that this new company should be capitalised to any larger extent than was likely to be necessary for further exploration of the concessions and for obtaining the best available advice from experts of high standing as to the prospective value of the areas held as a reasonable proposition for the production of a commercial supply of petroleum.

The result of this was that a new company, Timor Oil Limited, was formed with capital of £11,000 – 22,000 shares of 10/- each. Sir Joseph Carruthers remained chairman of the board of directors, with Arthur Staughton and Rutherford Affleck on the board. Sir Thomas Henley, a politician and prominent Sydney building contractor; and Sir Allen Taylor, a Sydney businessman and politician, later joined the board. Some years later, Henley was to have a very public row with Carruthers over the his (Henley's) book, *A Pacific Cruise* (Sydney, 1930).

In 1916 Benjamin Kendrick Stroud[52], an American oil expert 'of high repute', who had previously worked for the Standard Oil Company on their Californian oilfields, was hired to go to Timor to inspect the Timor Oil Limited's leases and concessions. He had been Superintendent of the Monte Cristo Oil and Development Company, Field Superintendent of the Universal Oil Company, and a part author, with Paul McClary Paine, of *Oil Production Methods*, published in San Francisco in 1913.

Stroud arrived in Sydney on 23rd May 1916 on the *Ventura*, along with his wife and daughter. He then left for Timor – because of the war, he went first to Java. He then returned to Australia, coming to Brisbane and from there went to Sydney on the *Wodonga*, wrote his report, and then went back to the United States on the *Ventura*. In his report in 1917 he noted:

> It is my opinion that the Company should carry on the work already started by adopting a consistent boring policy, and adhering to it until satisfied with results. I think three bores of 2000 feet each would probably be ample to test

---

[52] Benjamin Kendrick Stroud had been born on 4th March 1881 at Bakersfield, California, the son of John Allen Stroud and Mary (née Cole). His younger brother, John Allen Stroud jnr was worked at the University of California, Berkeley. Benjamin Stroud died on 2nd March 1950 in California.

the country – certainly there are surface evidences enough to justify the boring of at least three wells. These three bores could be placed No 1 at Vessoro, No 2 at Iribin, and No.3 at Atalele, unless better sites offer themselves as boring proceeds.

General Description:

The company's Concessions are on the Island of Timor, situated, about 400 miles NW of Port Darwin. The Island is about 300 miles long and averages about 40 miles wide. The Eastern half belongs to Portugal. The Concessions held by this Company are on the South Coast, about 45 miles from the eastern end of the Island. To reach the Concessions from Dilly, the capital and principal port, requires 35 hours of continuous horse-back riding. The distance is about 125 miles and the track traverses several mountain ranges. The island of Timor lies at the end of the Malay Archipelago and is similar geologically to the other islands of the group.

Java, Borneo and Sumatra are well known for their wonderful petroleum resources, and the Dutch Government has now practically stopped the further acquisition of lands by anyone other than the Government itself in order to control the output and price of petroleum.

To the east and south of Timor lie Australia and New Guinea. In the latter are many encouraging signs of oil, including mud volcanoes, gas blowouts and oil seepages, but the Commonwealth Government has withdrawn all lands from entry by private enterprise. Australia so far has not shown any indications whatever of oil, while it has been practically proved that there is no oil in New Zealand in commercial quantities. This leaves Timor as the one available place on which to prospect, with any hope of success, in an area covering the whole of Australasia and the Dutch East Indies. From the position of the Island one can easily see its vantage point as a producing centre with the East Indies and Australasia for markets. With the above in mind it is not hard to realise the value of the Concessions if once oil is found.

The Concessions.

Upon my arrival at Vessoro, I was met by Bryant, the Company's local agent, and with his help I inspected the tools, buildings and equipment. I found all the machinery in good condition, as Bryant had kept it well protected from the weather. Certain drilling tools were broken. I took a list of same so that duplicates or renewals could be made in Sydney.

I then turned my attention to the surface indications. Unfortunately a heavy storm during the previous week had covered the beach from three to five feet deep in sand, and the seepages were not as plainly developed as they would otherwise have been. However, I managed to see the oil oozing through the sand in five or six different places scattered over a radius of one hundred and fifty feet. The oil itself was light in gravity, of dark color, and no doubt contains a high percentage of petrol. From its color and fresh odor one could easily see that it had not migrated far from the parent body. The oil from the 32-ft. well was next examined. It is the same as the beach oil and shows up in good quantity considering its location to the seepage. The gas blow-out near the big rig is also another good indication; in fact, these evidences of petroleum are all from the Mete-Hou horizon-which outcrops at the beach-and although this horizon at this point is impoverished. due to its outcrop, it looks well for any lower oil zones that might be encountered.

The country around the Mete-Hou concessions has been more or less disturbed, and this may result in no oil from some bores, while others nearby will be prolific producers. It is hard to state whether this condition really exists without actual bore tests, but one should have such conditions in mind when boring on this property. Although seepages, gas blow-outs and the like are only guides and do not prove the existence of large bodies of oil, yet the indications at Vessoro are very encouraging and the Company is fully warranted in prospecting this concession with at least one 2000-ft. bore.

As regards location of bore, the plan 'A' of Foxall's report, 4/11/11, shows the present well to be 30 chains from the crest of the anticline as approximately marked by him. If this were the true crest of the anticline the well would appear to be badly placed, but I think liberal allowance can be made on both sides, although I do think the bore should have been started further to the East. As matters now stand, if the present bore can be carried on down, it would be advisable to do so if only for the knowledge of the territory to be used in later operations.

So far no information has come to hand regarding the condition of the bore. We know that it is 665-ft. deep, and that the casing is now 8-inch. We also know that certain difficulties were met with, but we do not know if they were overcome, and whether the bore is really clear for deepening. Mr W J McKeown, who drilled the well to the present depth, gave me a log of the formation in his letter of May 27th, 1917, but said nothing about condition of bore. I have written him since asking for details on the latter. In any event a competent driller could find out in a few days as to whether the hole could be deepened or not.

The Iribin concessions were next examined. These concessions, three in number, lie about 12 miles east of Vessoro. The track connecting Vessoro and

Iribin could easily be made into a road, over which heavy machinery could be hauled. The anticline cutting through these concessions would be my choice for the next bore site. The anticline itself seems gently folded, and not so broken looking as the Mete-Hou concessions of Vessoro. The Mete-Hou horizon here outcrops in the shape of gas blow-outs in three different places. The gas has an unmistakable petroleum smell.

North of Vessoro about four miles is Atalele, where two concessions are located. I did not visit Atalele owing to the condition of the trails. Two days after my arrival at Vessoro it started raining and kept it up every day during the remainder of my stay. I tried also to see Bibiluto, the outcrop of the lower horizon, 20 miles west of Vessoro, but the mud prevented our getting anywhere near it. In fact, Bryant stated that our trip was the hardest he had ever had on the Island...

Cost of Drilling in Timor

In order to study costs of drilling in Timor, it might be well to give a few comparative figures on operating conditions elsewhere. At present all oil men in America have been advanced 25 per cent. in wages and reduced from 12 hours to 8 hours per day, and making three drillers and three tool-dressers necessary where two of each were formerly used-a general all-round increase of over 35 per cent in wages alone. This would make drilling cost in California at least £2 per foot. In Java the wages paid to standard drillers is £40 per month to European drillers: £52 per month to American drillers. A house is furnished in addition to the foregoing, with water and fuel. The men board themselves at a cost of about £16 per man per month. Native labor – Well coolies 8d. per day; common coolies 4d. per day. Under ordinary running conditions in Sumatra, with the Canadian and Galacian system of drilling, the rate of progress for 78 wells was 3ft. per day (one shift), and the cost per foot for the 78 wells was £3/3/9. This figure includes sea and land transport, skilled and common labor, overhead charges, casing, rigs, machinery, etc. The wells were drilled in an average of about one year each; average depth being 1200ft. This figure of £3/3/9 could no doubt have been reduced by a better system of drilling. In fact, the territory in question is now being tried out by the rotary, but I do not know with what success.

The Commonwealth Government has spent over £60,000 upon their prospecting in Papua. They have a small production and the main bore is now 1,700ft. deep. Drilling has been done by standard tools here, but the rotary would do much better – that is make much faster time. From all reports this expenditure seems to be fully warranted.

In Timor where conditions are more or less unknown and must be learned, probably at considerable expense, the cost per foot will no doubt be high. It is not possible to make any previous estimate of expenditure under conditions of this kind, but one must prepare to meet unlikely contingencies.

After oil has been struck and the proposition proves to be commercially valuable, the following improvements would be in order:-

1. Roads and trails between important points.
2. Light rails and trucks for conveying materials.
3. Telephone system.
4. Pipe lines and laterals for gathering oil.
5. Tanks and earthen reservoirs for containing oil.
6. Camps at each of development areas.
7. Headquarters Camp.
8. Rest camp at high altitude with hospital.
9. Machine Shop, cold storage, plant, etc.
10. Saw Mill.
11. Brick Kilns.
12. Refinery with stills, agitators, tanks, etc., etc.
13. Delivery system to vessels, including loading platform in ocean.

Analysis of any of the above items would be out of place here, but it can be readily seen that the aggregate cost would be a large one. The question of a harbor on this island looks to be a serious one. For loading oil or refined products from tanks to ships, a quiet harbor where a loading wharf may be extended to deep water is very essential, not to mention the incoming cargo which must be taken care of and properly stored prior to being used. The map shows no such harbor nor did I talk with anyone who knew of a likely place. To load oil from shore to the boat lying at anchor in the ocean is not impossible, but the loading lines, floats, etc, are subject to very heavy strains at times, and may require frequent repair as well as costly initial installation.

Large versus Small Holdings

I have sketched roughly above what would be needed in equipping a plant should oil be found in Timor. For a holding of 2500 to 3500 acres this cost could easily total £600,000 to £750,000, or even more, considering the extra freight rates, duties. etc. (I refer to expenditure in peace times.) While spending such an amount of money, why not control as much oil-bearing land as possible? I am a firm believer in the pioneer getting the pick of the country. It will be found upon last analysis that the proved acreage is small enough. I have known of 30,000 prospective acres to dwindle down to 2500 acres proved oil-bearing land. In fact, the total proved acreage of the Californian oil-fields is very small compared with the original prospecting area. Therefore, I recommend that the Company be in a position previous to striking oil to ask the Portuguese Government for such an area, already chosen under the Portuguese Mining Law. This law states:- The Home Government may grant special license to prospect a certain portion of territory and to grant concessions without restrictions as to number of claims for the working on a large scale of a given mining zone. Were this area to be granted, the Company would then be in an excellent position so far as holdings are concerned. They could then lease, operate the property themselves, or sell their holdings outright.

As an example how oil holdings multiply out, let me give you the following: The total ultimate production per acre of several thousand acres in California was recently estimated by experts at 30,511 barrel per acre (1 barrel = 42 US gallons). Say the Timor fields, if oil is found, will average 10,000 barrels per acre. If the Company get 2000 acres of proved land out of their entire holdings, they would then have 20,000,000 barrels ultimate production. At 5/- per barrel this oil would have a value of £5,000,000, which, everything considered, would be a nominal value.

All the above, however, is contingent upon getting the oil in commercial quantities, and to this end all energy must be directed.

(Signed) B K Stroud

Stroud then offered to visit the United States to raise money for the project, eventually being authorized by the company to dispose of the Company's property on lease as follows:

(a) Thirty years' lease on a royalty of 10 per cent, of the gross product free of deduction over and above royalty payable to the Portuguese Government. [The royalty to the Portuguese government is .05 per cent.]
(b) Cash bonus for sale of tools and equipment £10,000,
(c) Usual agreements and covenants to protect the Company and ensure work being carried out expeditiously and to the satisfaction of the Company. Such agreements to be approved of by the Company's Attorneys in New York, whom it is proposed to appoint.
(d) Improvements on Company's areas to become the property of the Lessor subject to lease.

The slow-down and eventual stoppage of work during the last years of the First World War, and the regulations preventing transfers of money from Australia to East Timor meant that, despite the hopes of the investors, little progress was being made in extracting oil. In 1918 Sir Paul Chater, a Parsee businessman from Hong Kong, seemed ready to make an offer. However the Australian government intervened. Sir Joseph Carruthers had spoken to the Governor-General, Sir Ronald Munro-Ferguson, and it was decided that if Chater or some other Asian-based entity purchased the oil concessions, there was the real possibility of it ending up in Japanese hands – already deemed potentially hostile despite being an ally in the First World War. Certainly from even this time the Japanese were pursuing as many plans as possible to ensure a secure supply of oil. Admiral Jellicoe in London had suggested that the oilfields in Timor, if they did produce any sizeable quantity of oil might be used to supply the Royal Navy in Australian waters. This led to the involvement of the Anglo-Persian Oil Company in 1920. Arthur Staughton reported:

Arrived at Dilly 29th August, where we were met by our local representative, Mr G H Bryant, who introduced us to Mr Wilmoth, the representative and attorney of the Anglo-Persian Oil Company. Interviewed Governor. After a lot of consultations and much talk with his Chief of Staff, suspension from working conditions was granted until 30th June next (1921). Attended at Mines Department, found all titles in order and rents paid in advance.

After getting stores cleared from Customs, left for Bacau, where we arrived on the morning of 1st September. Arrived next day at Atalele and Iramuni concessions. After leaving called at a village adjoining called Leaseda. Spent two days here inspecting another oil seep about a mile from our boundary. Both Dr Wade[53] and Mr Wilmoth were much impressed with these shows. Next left for our headquarters at Vessoro. On arrival there found all machinery in first-class order. Dr Wade was greatly impressed with the completeness of our outfit, which, subject to slight repairs, was practically in a condition to start work straightaway.

We next heard of oil indications on the eastern and western sides of our Mete-Hou Concessions, and decided to extend our areas if possible. Both geologists were taken with the numerous outbreaks of oil, gas and bitumen and

---

[53]    Arthur Wade, born 1878 in Halifax, Yorkshire, England; educated at Royal College of Science, University of London; involved in search for oil in Papua New Guinea in 1913; later settled in Western Australia; died 1951 in Queensland.

especially with the geographical structures of the rock formation on these concessions which all indicated a big oil supply.

Next visited our Iribin Concessions, the geology of which are touched upon by Dr Wade in his preliminary report. Stayed here four days in order to give these Concessions a good overhaul. Returned to Vessoro on the 15th September. Left for Dilly on the 16th, arriving there on the 22nd. Dr Wade here furnished me with his preliminary report and left by Dutch boat for Sourabaya on the 23rd. Left for the mountains overlooking the town to await the return of the Governor, who was away inspecting the western portion of the Island. Interviewed him on his return with regard to an extension of our Concessions, which can only be granted by direct application, through the British Authorities, to Lisbon, Portugal.

Before leaving arranged for Senor Armando de Barros to act as the Company's representative. Cannot speak too highly of the manner in which this gentleman treated me both on my arrival and return to Dilly, being most hospitably entertained by him.

Left per s.s. *Montoro* on Wednesday, 6th October, arriving at Sydney on Wednesday, 20th October.

Furthermore Dr Wade noted:

Titles: I have examined the documents relating to titles in the Mines Department at Dilly, and find them to be in order. Three of the areas are definitely granted as Concessions, the remaining four are manifested and from my interpretation of the Portuguese Mining Law, they must be granted as soon as a definite request is made. Rent on the first three areas is paid up to date. and for the next twelve months. No rent is paid on the remaining areas, but must be paid as soon as concession rights are definitely asked for and granted. Was present at an interview with the Governor, during which he promised to extend the period of the concessions to the end of June 1921. Saw the request for such extension written and handed in officially to the proper quarter.

Extension of Concessions: Iramuni and Atalele – I do not advise any extension at present. Irabin and Bualiu – These areas are large and need not be extended at present…

Negotiations with the Anglo-Persian Oil Company came to nought. And in 1920 the Timor Oil Company, unable to locate any sizeable deposits of oil, requested for an extension of the areas in which they were allowed to prospect, particularly the area around Mete-Hou. The Portuguese government seemed happy to entertain this as news came in of a reported oil strike in Portuguese East Africa (Mozambique). The land leased to the Timor Oil Company was enlarged in 1923, but at the same time the Timor Development Company appeared on the scene.

The Timor Development Company was run by Samuel Jacobs, a South Australian businessman who wanted to use British and Australian capital to develop the untapped potential of East Timor. Specialising in (or strictly speaking, planning to specialise in) coffee and cotton, in 1928 the Timor Development Company was reportedly having trouble securing titles to agricultural property, and in the following year seems to have either pulled out or restricted itself to a small-scale import-export business. There seems to have been limited harassment of some British subjects around this time, and the (unrelated) death on 2nd April 1928 of the Anglo-Australian geologist, Captain Leonard Langdale Wrathall.

Wrathall had been in Timor for a few years and was 'in charge of boring operations for oil' for the Timor Petroleum Company Limited. Born in 1893 at Steeton, Yorkshire (West Riding), England, the son of Charles Wrathall, the manager of John Clough & Sons' spinning worsted mill, he had attended Keighley Boys' Grammar School from where he gained a minor scholarship which he used to study metallurgy at the Royal School of Mines in London 1909–13. As soon as his course finished, he accepted a position with the Australian Government and went to Australia and then to Papua where he had been involved in geological work with Ernest Sterne Usher, possibly the search for oil there – Usher died in Port Moresby in September 1916[54]. Wrathall, then moved to Sydney and married Nell M Williams at Mosman, Sydney in 1915.

On 1st October 1915 Wrathall enlisted in the Australian Army joining the 3rd Reinforcements of the Mining Corps and sailing on 4th April 1916 on the *Euripides*. His enlistment papers note his previous occupation as 'geologist', and his place of residence at the time of enlistment as being Neutral Bay, New South Wales. His next of kin was his wife (address: 'c/o Bank of New South Wales, London').

Serving in the Gallipoli campaign, Wrathall was involved in the mining of Hill 60 in August 1915.[55] Two years later, while on active service in France he was injured by shrapnel which wounded him in the face, Wrathall

---

[54]   R K Johns, *History and role of government geological surveys in Australia*, Adelaide: Government Printer, 1976.
[55]   *The Keightley News* 21 April 1917, p. 3; 19 May 1928, p. 6.

Leonard Wrathall (front row, seated, third from left) with the 2nd Australian Tunnelling Company, on the roadside near Querrieu, France, 1st April 1918.

convalesced in London before returning to northern France, and in 1918 was Mentioned in Despatches. After the war Wrathall returned to work as a geologist initially with the Anglo-Persian Oil Company. He seems to already have established some reputation for searching for oil when working with Anglo-Persian, before he moved to Timor where he was Field Superintendent and Geologist for the Timor Petroleum Company Limited. He died from blackwater fever on 2nd April 1928,[56] and there was a major commotion when his widow claimed that she was ill-treated by the Portuguese court which 'declined to admit her identity or status [and] refused to hand over to her any of her husband's property and had with difficulty been dissuaded from selling the whole of the deceased gentleman's effects by auction'.[57] Wrathall was described in an obituary as being 'a man

---

[56] His probate papers, issued in 1933, list 'Portuguese Timor' as place of residence. See also the brief mention of his death in *The Argus* 7 April 1928, p. 18.

[57] 'Case of Mrs Wrathall', Australian CRS A981: item Portuguese Timor 17, quoted by Peter Hastings, *op.cit.* Mrs Wrathall married Hinton Louis Wills in 1932 in Redfern. Wills died in 1943 at Chatswood.

of high attainments and unassuming manner'.[58] He is believed to have been buried in the Protestant Section of the Santa Cruz Cemetery in Dili, and is commemorated on his parents' gravestone in the churchyard of St Stephen's Steeton, Yorkshire. There was a brief death notice in *The Times* on 18th May 1928.

---

[58]    *The Keightley News* 19 May 1928, p. 6.

## CHAPTER FOUR

In 1926 the Portuguese Republic, established in 1910, collapsed and after a coup, Salazar became Minister of Finance (and Premier of Portugal six years later). The stability that Salazar brought to Lisbon politics meant that there was an increased interest in the search for oil in East Timor. On 25th October 1926 Arthur Staughton seemed to have breathed fresh life into the Timor Oil Company. His first move seemed to have been to establish a new company, the Timor Petroleum Company, based in Melbourne, which purchased seven leases from the Timor Oil Company. This new company arranged some test drilling in Timor, and the results were obviously fruitful enough to restart the search for oil.

In an attempt to establish which concessions had been made, and which had not, and to whom, Stanley Bruce, the Australian Prime Minister, asked the British Ambassador in Lisbon, Sir Lancelot Carnegie, to try to ascertain the existing situation. The Portuguese government, who also seemed to be a little unclear on what had been leased, and to whom, managed to clarify which concessions were owned by the Timor Petroleum Company. These seem to have been on favourable terms – that is favourable to the Australians[59] – and hence when, in July 1927 the Portuguese decided to ask for tenders for a monopoly on oil concessions in East Timor, those areas held by the Timor Petroleum Company were exempted – these are what became known as the Staughton Concession. However Staughton seems to have been cautious about spending any more money extending the leases he already held until some oil had been found, and this caution resulted in

---

[59]   This seems to have been the grant of 4,000 acres in perpetuity.

another company, Australian Oilfields Company, thought by the Australian Government to be under German control, also to hold back.

By 1929 the Timor Petroleum Company was running into serious difficulties, and the Anglo-Portuguese (Timor) Development Syndicate was established 'to exploit mining and trading concessions'. This syndicate was short-lived and does not seem to have made any advance in search for oil or other minerals, and there were allegations of fraud made against the directors.

In 1932 as fresh rumours for the sale of East Timor, this time to the Japanese resurfaced. On 10th October, a London newspaper alleged that the Japanese had made approaches to buy East Timor but this was flatly denied by the Japanese Embassy in London two days later.[60] This new rumour came about as the Timor Petroleum Company went into liquidation and the Timor Oil Company was formed. The main asset of this new company was continued control over the Staughton Concession. In 1936 the British Foreign Office decided, on advice from the Anglo-Iranian Oil Company (formerly the Anglo-Persian Oil Company) that the commercial value of the Staughton Concession was 'slight'. At this point a new player appeared on the scene.

In June 1936 the Allied Mining Corporation of Manila[61] claimed to have negotiated with the Portuguese government for an oil concession covering the whole of East Timor. In fact there had been five applications for the sole right to prospect in East Timor – and four of these had come from Japanese companies. The Allied Mining Corporation was headed by Dr Serge F Wittouck, a Belgian financier who seemed to have lost a fortune in France with a scheme to turn coal into oil, and an American, Mr Houghton, described by Rev Sir Henry Fitzmaurice, the British Consul-General in Batavia as 'being a dubious character'.[62] Wittouck was, in July 1938, to argue that the Allied Mining Corporation was a British company registered in Hong Kong.[63]

---

[60]    *The Times* 13 October 1932, p. 13.
[61]    'Allied Mining Corporation, 509 Insular Life Building', *Manila Telephone Directory*, June 1940, p. 4.
[62]    FO 371/21041.
[63]    *Documents on Australian Foreign Policy, op.cit.,* Vol 1, p. 392.

This development created great concern in Australia where the Timor Oil Company was about to sell off its assets (namely the Staughton Concession) to a new company, Anglo-Eastern Oil Company. A representative of the Anglo-Eastern Oil Company, C J Manning[64], quickly ensured that the £125 annual payment to the Timor authorities for the lease was made, and as the funds had been accepted by the authorities in Dili, he regarded the Staughton Concession as still extant. The full force of the British and Australian consular and diplomatic department came into force. Keith Officer, Commonwealth of Australia External Affairs Officer in London, and Rex Cullen-Ward[65], the Portuguese Consul in Sydney since 1924, both sent off telegrams to Lisbon and Dili respectively, and Charles E Critchley, the Australian Trade Commissioner in Batavia, also sought to find whether the Staughton Concession still existed and claimed to have been held by two Australian companies, Oil Search and Oil Concessions No Liability. The British Foreign Office reported that 'the Portuguese are probably quite equal to selling the same mining rights to several different parties'.

The British Consul-General in Manila, Stanley Wyatt-Smith, also sought out Dr Wittouck to find if there were any Japanese interests in his company. Wittouck assured them that there was not. However there was a German connection through Max Sander, a German Jew who had lived in East Timor since before the First World War. He had lost his German nationality when he failed to turn up for military service in 1914. As he was Jewish, there seemed little likelihood of Nazi German involvement.

Owing to what must have seemed like the inordinate number of changes in ownership of the Staughton Concession in Australia, the Timor authorities still had the Concession registered in the name of Arthur Staughton, and declared that this would be cancelled as the Allied Mining Corporation of Manila had made an application unless the £125 was paid (again). However the Portuguese Foreign Minister then assured the British that the Staughton Concession was not threatened but should not be used to stop other companies. In January 1937 it was reported that 'practically no work' had

---

[64]    He would appear to be Cyril Joseph Manning who was born in Carlton on 1st January 1903, and enlisted as a Private, 2/2 Pioneer Battalion, Australian Infantry, on 3rd June 1940. He was held as a Japanese prisoner of war in Java and then transported to work on the Burma-Siam Railway where he died on 27th July 1943, aged 40. He was buried in Kanchanaburi War Cemetery, Thailand (Collective Grave 1 Q 2–78).

[65]    Grandfather of Susan Cullen Ward who, in 1975, married Leka I, exiled King of the Albanians.

been done on the Staughton Concession for 'about eight years'. Thus Wittouck, who claimed to have spent £50,000 in exploration work (and thus for whom the extra payment of $$125 should not have been a problem), seemed to be able to start work with plans to exploit oil and mineral resources and also plant crops over some 25,000 hectares. However without the Staughton Concession, he controlled only 1,500 square miles.

By now it seems to many seasoned observers that there was little prospect of anybody party finding much oil or minerals in Timor, whoever controlled the Staughton Concession. With Salazar in control in Lisbon, there was also little likelihood of East Timor being sold to anybody. Thus attention in East Timor focused on worries that the Japanese were making inroads into area. That Japanese business and Japanese military intelligence went hand-in-hand is well known. And thus when it was reported that, in June 1937 it emerged that the Nanyo Kohatsu Kaisha [South Seas Development Company] had been formed in Tokyo, as had the Japanese-Portuguese Development Company (capital: 5 million yen), both Australian and British governments took notice. Although some people have seen the Australian and British concern largely over fears that the Japanese would dominate economically, and force out Australian and/or British companies, the political (and military) fear was more important. Indeed with the exception of the failed mining ventures, the major Australian and British money to be invested in East Timor was solely to ensure that the Japanese faced stiff competition.

The Japanese certainly had plans for East Timor and they received a jolt when the HMS *Folkestone* visited Dili in November 1936. The Timor authorities had maintained that there were no Japanese activities in East Timor. However rumours did circulate that this visit was the prelude to a British takeover, although the Portuguese Governor of East Timor did go to Batavia to explain that this was not the case.

Although the statement that there were no Japanese activities in East Timor when the HMS *Folkestone* visited, it seems that the visit was the catalyst for the Japanese to start their commercial expansion into East Timor. In July 1937 it emerged that some Japanese were negotiating to purchase some 20 square miles which belonged to Montalvao da Silva, son of Celestino da Silva (who was Governor of Portuguese Timor 1894–1908). The price, was variously put at 4 million yen or 2 million guilders. In addition, as Wittouck seemed not to have found anything to mine, there was the genuine possibility that he might sell his leases to the Japanese. Thus the Australians were eager to ensure that the Staughton Concession still existed, not for what might be found there, but to keep the Japanese out. The British sounded out Wittouck again and he stated that he was not going to sell out to the Japanese. The British Consul-General in Batavia added a *caveat*: 'I am unable to rely greatly on Mr S F Wittouck's statements, although much of his information is of great interest as casting a little more light into the dark corners of shady Portuguese Timor'.

Then to confuse things even further, there was a fresh flurry of rumours suggesting that the Portuguese government were offering East Timor for sale to either Australia or to the British in 1938. This new wave of rumours seems to have originated from Athol Stuart, general manager of Fairfax newspapers 1933–38. On his resignation, on medical grounds, in August 1938, he led an Australian government-backed expedition to the Northern Territory and to Java, and whilst there seemed to have come across latent rumours about the possible sale of East Timor, and was overheard by the British Consul in Batavia making remarks about this. He was later confined to a lunatic asylum[66] However this time the British Foreign Office decided that in relation to the possible purchase, 'before this project is definitively shelved, some authoritative opinion should be obtained of the strategic utility of Timor to the Empire'. In a note from the British Admiralty marked 'Secret' and dated 11th October 1938, J H Phillips wrote to the Under-Secretary of State at the Foreign Office:

Sir,

I am commanded by My Lords Commissioners of the Admiralty, to acquaint you for the information of the Secretary of State for Foreign Affairs... concerning a suggestion that Portuguese Timor might be purchased by Great Britain or Australia.

After consideration of the information at their disposal, My Lords have reached the conclusion that it is most improbable that Portugal would at the present time wish to dispose of this colony, either to this country or to the Netherlands, *who have the first option.*[67] [my italics] There appears to be no real danger that Portugal would consider selling to Japan without first approaching the Netherlands and Great Britain.

---

[66]    The *Australian Dictionary of Biography* (Vol 12, p. 127) states his confinement took place in January 1942, but British Foreign Office correspondence dated 4th October 1938 note that it had already taken place. See also Gavin Souter, *Company of Heralds*, Carlton: Melbourne University Press, 1981.

[67]    In a Foreign Office memo dated 2nd November 1938 the British urge that 'should Portuguese Government wish to relinquish the territory, Dutch Government should be encouraged to exercise their option of purchase'.

The immediate need seems therefore to be for Japanese penetration in the colony by the extension of Japanese commerce and interests to be resisted; but My Lords feel that the Portuguese Government have done, and are doing all they could reasonably be asked to do in this direction, and it would be difficult to urge them to take a stronger line unless perhaps British interests were now prepared to give financial support to the development of the colony.

Three weeks later, the British Air Ministry reiterated that everything should be done to prevent the Japanese getting a toehold in East Timor but that there would be little benefit to Britain 'from an air aspect by the acquisition of this territory'. The result of these soundings, including whether Germany might make a claim on Timor based on the 1898 Agreement, convinced the British Government that if Portugal retained control of East Timor, a *status quo* would be satisfactory for British and Australian interests. However the real focus of attention was in increasing Japanese interests in Timor. A paper from the British War Office, dated 2nd November 1938, and marked 'Secret' noted:

The [Army] Council consider that a Japanese occupation of Timor would constitute no new direct threat to Singapore which, though the distance is somewhat greater, would be more easily attacked by the Japanese from Formosa [Taiwan].

The only direct threat would appear to be to Australia. In the Council's view, however, Great Britain might be indirectly affected in the following ways:

(a)  Such a threat to Australia might deter the Australian Government from sending troops to reinforce British forces in other theatres of war.

(b)  In paragraphs 50-52 of COS 710 the possibility was considered of Australia, in the event of war, flying air reinforcements to Singapore. Whilst this is primarily an Air Ministry matter, it would seem that if Portuguese Timor became a British possession such reinforcement might be considerably facilitated whilst serious interference might be caused should the territory be occupied by the Japanese

It is therefore the opinion of the Council that, whilst Australia is most directly concerned, Great Britain might derive some strategical advantage from the denial of Portuguese Timor to the Japanese and possibly from its inclusion in the British Empire.

The Japanese aims were quickly emerging. With their (planned) increased trade, they were offering to enlarge Dili harbour, build godowns along the port and 'before long, obtain a permanent hold on that colony (sic) analogous to the position she has achieved at Davao, Mindanao. The Nanyo Kohatsu Kaisha has already indicated in New Guinea and elsewhere its readiness to undertake agricultural, mineral and fishery enterprises even when profits are problematical.'[68] This meant that the Australians and/or the British had to stop the Japanese from either buying Wittouck's concessions or acquiring the Société Agricole, a Timorese company which held much land on the island. Certainly Wittouck himself would welcome a possible unofficial 'auction' between the Australians and the Japanese of his assets on the island which do not seem to have returned much for his investment. However an easier solution for the Australians was to rework the Staughton Concession, and ensure that it was still valid.

By August 1937 the Australian Government had provided grants for E J Pascoe, a former director of Oil Search Ltd, to go to Portuguese Timor in the hope that he might actually find oil, but even if he did not, he would re-establish the Staughton Lease.[69] With a new Governor of Portuguese Timor having been appointed, Rev Sir Henry Fitzmaurice, Britain's Consul-General in Batavia, sought information from J K Stephenson, an Irishman who had lived in Portuguese Timor since 1924 and had worked, briefly, for the Asia Investment Company. They received permission from Salazar to prospect for mineral oils and hydro-carbon gases east of the meridian 125° 50' – it had been possible for immense Australian pressure to prove that Wittouck was a share (or land) speculator, whereas the Australians were actually keen on developing the mineral resources of the island. Coupled with the Portuguese authorities bringing in legislation which would effectively deny the Japanese the ability to establish any large concession, the Australian plans seemed to be working. The British Vice-Consul to Batavia, Edward Lambert[70] then visited Dili to start plans to establish a British consular post there. The visit by the Dutch Governor of the Netherlands East Indies in 1938 finally seemed to squash ideas that East Timor might be 'up for sale'.

The Japanese then tried a new tactic to try to get control of East Timor. They were unable to set up their own concession, they were thwarted from buying the Wittouck leases, and had failed to persuade the Portuguese

---

[68]    FO 371/21041.
[69]    *Documents on Australian Foreign Policy, op.cit.* Vol 1, p. 185.
[70]    Born on 19th June 1901, and died in May 1994 at Deben, Suffolk.

authorities of their bona fides in a proposed purchase of the Société Agricole. They had only one other card to play – that was by putting pressure on Macao which they disliked because much of the smuggling into China seemed to emanate from there.[71] The pressure could then be relaxed if the Portuguese allowed the Japanese to use Dili as a port for their steamship line. Portugal had, itself, only one ship in Timorese waters. This was the *Dili*, formerly a US Coast and Geodetic Survey vessel used in the Philippines. It had been sold when the Americans thought it obsolete, and the *Dili* now made monthly trips around East Timor and the Okusi enclave, as well as collecting in the coffee crop and other food. It was probably the same vessel which Staughton called *Dilly* when he visited East Timor in 1912.

With the Japanese exercising pressure through the Portuguese keen to keep trade going in Macao, the Australians and the British seemed unable to manage to keep Japan excluded. The joint Portuguese-Japanese company, the Timor Archipelago Development Company (Timor Gunto Kaihatsu Kaisha) was formed to develop the lands of the Société Agricole, particularly expand its coffee production. The Australian government then

decided to re-open talks about using Dili as a possible air route. The plan was for Hudson Fysh (left), Managing Director of the Queensland and Northern Territories Air Services (Qantas) to gain an air concession in Dili.[72] As Alfred Stirling, Australian External Affairs Officer in London, wrote, on 30th October 1937:

It was pointed out that the proposal to include Dili in the Qantas Empire Airways route between Singapore and Darwin might conveniently be linked with the other suggestion now on foot for an extension of Australian influence in Portuguese Timor, namely development of the Staughton oil concession. The view was expressed that if the hoped-for exploitation of the concession went through, the Commonwealth Government might find that the logical consequence was the development also of communications with Portuguese Timor.[73]

---

[71]  See also *The Times* 23 October 1941, p. 3.
[72]  Sir Hudson Fysh. *Qantas at War*, Sydney: Angus & Robertson, 1968, p. 112.
[73]  *Documents on Australian Foreign Policy, op.cit.* Vol 1, p. 224.

Against this was the obvious geographical fact that if Kupang was used instead of Dili, the route would be about 75 miles shorter. There was a hope that the British might take up what would obviously be an unprofitable route but by March 1939 Imperial Airways had found it impractical to include Dili on its Flying Boat Service.[74] Soon even the Australians were holding off, in the seemingly vain hope that something might be found to be found in the Staughton Concession.[75] In fact the Japanese seemed keen on establishing their own air base, and, for the British, with events in Europe taking priority over Asian affairs, the Australians rapidly felt being left on their own in trying to persuade the Portuguese to keep out the Japanese. The British argued that their own naval forces from Singapore could easily outpace the Japanese and 'a fleet based on Singapore would endanger the long and vulnerable lines of communications of a Japanese expedition against Australia, and it is most improbable that the Japanese, taking this fact into consideration, would ever embark on such an operation'.[76]

Whilst the British seemed content, the Australians remained nervous. At the start of July 1939 the Australian Government decided to send James V Fairbairn, Minister for Civil Aviation, to Dili 'by Lockheed aeroplane landing at Dili, or if Dili unsuitable, landing Koepang [Kupang] and proceeding by road to Dilli'.[77] Luckily there were landing facilities at Dili, because the road between the two towns, would have necessitated a very long journey by car. In fact the airport at Dili had been built with British help. Jock Wilson, from Ipoh in Malaya, had worked on the construction of some of the airport terminal. He died in Dili and was buried in the Protestant section of the Santa Cruz Cemetery.[78]

The visit passed off well with Fairbairn being flown into Dili by Captain E C Johnston on a Guinea Airways Lockheed VH-AAU aircraft. Also involved in the journey were Captain D G Cameron, with David Ross

[74]    *ibid*, Vol 2, p. 61.
[75]    *ibid*, Vol 2, p. 64.
[76]    *ibid*, Vol 2, p. 95.
[77]    *ibid*, p. 146. See also *The Times* 19 July 1939, p. 13; 25 July 1939, p. 11.
[78]    I am grateful to Mary Russell for this information.

The Empire flying-boat over Dili harbour

as the navigator and E D Scott[79] operating the radio. Cameron had competed against Ross and many others in the Brisbane-Adelaide Air Race of 1934, with Ross was later to return to Dili as the Australia's unofficial representative.

Johnston's first comments seem to have been that the aerodrome was unsuitable for regular use but that the water seemed good for flying-boats. Sir Hudson Fysh noted in his book, *Qantas at War*, that aviation journalist Jack Percival, on seeing Dili wrote: 'I felt sorry I did not have enough money to buy it and present it to a national museum as a relic of the 16th century'.[80]

With the outbreak of war in Europe in September 1939, events in East Timor were given a low priority for a short period, even by the Australian Government. However as defence planning started in earnest, the Australians were still uncertain how the Staughton Concession stood vis-à-vis the Wittouck concession. The Portuguese Minister, Dr Machado, finally conceded that Wittouck had 'moral rights' which might have to be

---

[79]    Ernest Scott, born in 1913 was educated at Melbourne Grammar School 1924–32 and the University of Melbourne. Joining the Royal Australian Air Force in 1933, he transferred to New Guinea Airways as a pilot in 1939 and rejoined the RAAF during the Second World War. Captured by the Japanese at Ambon, he died whilst a prisoner of war on 6th February 1942.

[80]    Sir Hudson Fysh. *Qantas at War*, *op.cit.*, p. 112. It was not until the 1960s that there was a small air service operating out of Timor – Transportes Aéros de Timor which used a Douglas DC–3 between Baucau and Darwin.

purchased. In October 1939 the Australians finally decided to rework the Staughton Concession, obviously to keep out the Japanese and ensure that there were a number of Australians in the area, and that the Australian government would indemnify Wittouck against anything being found there.[81] This was certainly an odd arrangement given that the Australians had always believed, or been led to believe, that the Staughton Concession was fully valid – 'in perpetuity' as the original lease agreements stated. However on another level the indemnity was not that important, financially. Nothing seems ever to have been found in either the Staughton or Wittouck concessions, and national security was paramount. A new company, called Oil Concessions was established.

In November 1939 it was learned from intelligence sources in Lisbon that the Japanese were still keeping up the pressure on the Portuguese.[82] However by then the Australian company, Oil Concessions Limited had formed a Portuguese subsidiary, Ultramarina de Petroleos. The Japanese were furious and immediately redoubled their pressure on Macao, at which point the Portuguese then took a legalistic stance insisting that whilst the Australian interests were obeying the terms of their lease, nothing could be done about it. At this point the Japanese put on pressure from a new direction. Sir Robert Craigie, the British Ambassador to Japan, wrote to London and urged that the Japanese be allowed to take part in the search for oil with the Australians. Craigie felt that the new Japanese government under General Abe was moderate and was deeply wounded by the Nazi-Soviet Pact of August 1939[83]. Thus he urged for Britain to make conciliatory gestures towards Japan. Craigie's advice was rejected out-of-hand. The situation on the ground had also become easier for the Staughton Concession with the death, in Manila in July 1940 of Serge Wittouck.

A British scheme was then floated by which Anglo-Iranian and Royal Dutch Shell might take over the Staughton Concession. However Oil Concessions demanded too high a price in some forlorn hope that oil might be found. Unable to pay to keen hold of the lease, the Australian government injected an initial £12,000 to ensure the lease did not lapse.[84] Soon afterwards news was released in Tokyo that the Japanese Ministry of

---

[81]    *ibid*, p. 300 & 306.
[82]    *ibid*, p. 396.
[83]    Sir Robert Craigie, *Behind the Japanese Mask*, London: Hutchinson, 1945, Chapter 14.
[84]    Glyn Stone, *op.cit.,* p. 186.

QANTAS EMPIRE AIRWAYS LTD.

FIRST OFFICIAL AUSTRALIAN AIR MAIL
SERVICE PORTUGUESE TIMOR-AUSTRALIA.

Primeira
mala aérea directa de
Dili para Austrália

Hudson Fysh Esq.,
Qantas Empire Airways Ltd.,
Box 489AA. G.P.O.,
SYDNEY. N.S.W. AUSTRALIA.

IF NOT DELIVERED WITHIN 14 DAYS
RETURN TO BOX 489 AA. SYDNEY

Capt. *RW Tapp* R.M.A. "Cambria"
G-ADUV.

---

QANTAS EMPIRE AIRWAYS LTD.

FIRST AUSTRALIA-PORTUGUESE TIMOR
AIR MAIL SERVICE 17.1.41.

2
NOT
OPENED BY
CENSOR

Capt. *HB Hussey*
G-AETV "Coriolanus"

Mr. I.O.Lawson,
c/o Mr. C.W.Nielson, Representative,
Qantas Empire Airways Limited,
DILI.
PORTUGUESE TIMOR.

IF NOT DELIVERED WITHIN 14 DAYS
RETURN TO BOX 489 AA. SYDNEY

FIRST FLIGHT. By flying boat."Coriolanus." C.AETV."
SYDNEY - DILLI. Capt.H.B.Hussey.
PORTUGUESE TIMOR.
BY QANTAS EMPIRE AIRWAYS.

BY AIR MAIL
PAR AVION

RS
SYDNEY U
NEW SOUTH WALES
No. 9846

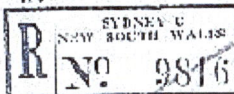

THE AIR MAIL
SOCIETY OF N.S.W.

MR.E.A.CROSS.
C/o QANTAS EMPIRE AIRWAY
DILLI.PORTUGUESE TIMOR.

Pilot. HB Hussey.
If not claimed within 7 days please return to
43 Enmore Rd., Newtown, N.S.W.

AIR MAIL
AR AVION

Opened by Censor

est Airmail Service -
Australia to Portugese Timor.

Mr. I. R. Hodder,

C/- Chef de Postes,

D I L L I,

PORTUGESE TIMOR.

HB Hussey

PASSED BY
CENSOR

V99

Finance had put aside 50,000 yen to establish a consulate at Dili. The British had urged the Australians to do the same. When the Australians did not initially do anything, the British in February 1940 confirmed the appointment made in December of the previous year of Henry Walsh as British 'Consul-General for the Netherlands East Indies, with the exception of the Province of East Java and the Province of Sumatra, to reside at Batavia; and to be also His Majesty's Consul-General for Portuguese Timor'.[85]

On 3rd October 1940, Captain Russell Brooke Tapp flew to Dili on the Qantas flying boat *Corinna*. Prominent 'aerophilatelist' and stamp collector E A Crome did manage to get Tapp to carry twelve postal covers (envelopes with stamps, but no letter) with the message: 'By first connecting flight from Australia: Sydney-Darwin-Koepang-Dilli-Portuguese Timor.' It is not known what Tapp did on the trip, which seems to have been to see about the possibility for Qantas flying to Dili, but he returned with the letters which were then posted from Newtown, NSW. The flight only reached public attention when two covers from the flight were sold at auction in 1992.[86]

The Tapp flight was followed, on 22nd October 1940, by the first of six agreed Japanese survey flights into Dili from their bases in Palau. Their aircraft, a four-engine Dornier flying-boat owned by Dai Nippon Airways, landed outside the reef and taxied into Dili harbour where the Japanese hosted a massive party for all and sundry.

Also on 22nd October, in the British, and representatives from India, Australia and New Zealand met in Singapore for the First Singapore Conference to discuss defence plans should Japan attack. With Japanese flights becoming a reality, it was left to the Australians to step up their involvement in Timor. On 29th December 1940 David Ross returned to Timor for a special four day mission to East Timor. This essentially resulted in an agreement between the Australian and Portuguese governments for landing rights for British and Australian planes at Dili. The flights were arranged by John McEwen who had taken over as Minister of Civil Aviation – James Fairbairn had been killed in an air-crash at Canberra in August.[87]

---

[85]     *London Gazette* 23 February 1940; *The Times* 24 February 1940, p. 8.
[86]     Charles Leski & Associates, *Airmails IV Auction*, 9th December 1992, lots 528–29.
[87]     Arthur Fadden was appointed Minister for Air on Fairbairn's death. McEwen was appointed in charge of civil aviation in October 1940.

Sir Hudson Fysh wrote affectionately about the arranging of flights to Dili. Staying at the Portugal Hotel there, a power cut greeted his first visit with André de la Porte, a Dutch aviation official. He wrote:

The electrical supply, it appeared, functioned only at times; and, when it did, most of the current was dissipated through leakage, places at a distance receiving only enough to produce a dull glow in the light filaments. The wiring was most haphazard and in places attached roughly to trees. The ice-plant had ceased for want of ammonia, and there were no refrigerators and no fans. We were told that luxuries of this sort just did not exist owing to lack of money to buy them, a fact which we were to verify during our week's stay.

Despite its dilapidated state and broken-down old-world colonial atmosphere Dili at one time with its cathedral, large public buildings, well-laid-out streets, and waterfront promenade where the polite local native dandies took the air in the evening, must have been quite a place. Today the town had a primitive broken-down appearance relieved by the curving beach of the harbour and the huge tropical trees behind which towered a background of high hills. That evening as André and I sat out in front of the hotel in the darkness we were treated to a great fireworks display by the fireflies, snapping their star-like little lights on and off as they flew about and returned to a tree which must have been their headquarters and was ablaze with them. My diary reads:

*Heat, heat. Not a tremor even on the tops of the tallest trees where the moonlight filters through. A terrific stillness descends on everything. You could feel it. The 9 o'clock curfew for the natives is in force.*

*We turn in. Windows tightly shuttered Portuguese fashion despite the great heat. A stone is rolled against the hotel front door as the latch is broken.*

*Awake in the early morning the enveloping stillness is still there. With the first streak of dawn a dog howls. A cock crows. Some strange birds call and suddenly the whole dense leafy arbour of our tropical surroundings breaks out in a sudden babel of sound as a myriad birds chatter and welcome the day.*

I found meals at the Portugal Hotel quite an entertainment, though towards the end of my stay I descended to eating almost exclusively lightly boiled eggs and bananas as I could not get used to the food.

At our first breakfast I noticed each guest carried in with him or her a large flagon of Portuguese wine which was carefully placed alongside the chair ready to be raised and tilted over the arm into large drinking glasses. A dowager made her stately entrance with her daughter hanging on her arm in old-world courtier style. This was Portuguese Timor, and even the natives courteously raised their hands in greeting when met on the street. This was Church influence. But in that wretched hotel no one spoke English or Malay – which made things very awkward.

My interview next morning was at the Residency with the Portuguese Governor, His Excellency Manuel d'Abreu Ferreira de Carvalho. I was well and courteously received and every assistance was extended. I met Abilio Augusto Monteiro da Amaral, Chief of Customs, and then paid a visit to the Chief of Posts and Telegraphs, Fortunato Mourao, in a large, old, and dilapidated Post Office building. As I sat in his office swallows flew in and out through the top of a glassless window and tended their nest built in the high comer of the room – he was a bird-lover indeed. We discussed airmail arrangements over a cup of the delightful local coffee. Next, round at Dili's only bank, the Banco Nacional Ultramarino, I met the Director, Jorge Duarte, who agreed that the bank would act as our agents. Meanwhile André had been busy and had contacted a Chinaman, one Loja A Jong, who owned a decrepit motorboat which he agreed to hire as a refuelling barge.

All now seemed in readiness for the first service. I got a short cable away to Head Office in Sydney which cost me 209 petakas – £16 6sh 7d.! I was informed by the Governor later that all the colony got out of it was 13 petakas, the rest going to satisfy Dutch and Australian charges and the conversion of petakas into guilders and Australian pounds. The colony of course just had no foreign credit and was ripe for exploitation or assistance, whatever you like to call it – which was being supplied by the forward-looking Japanese.

At last the great day for Dili arrived when it was going to have its regular fortnightly contact with the outside world by Empire flying-boat, and on 19th January 1941 *Coriolanus*, in command of Captain Hussey, slanted down out of the skies and alighted on the harbour, turning and taxiing up to our mooring laid about eighty yards from the Japanese mooring.

While this was happening I was at the Residency interviewing the Governor on some last-minute matters and arranging for him and his daughter to come aboard and inspect the boat. In the midst of the audience an attendant came in and handed me a very sodden piece of paper on which I could just read: 'Refuelling launch broken down send help – André'. There was a dripping native standing outside. He had dived overboard from the drifting launch and swum ashore with the note held between his teeth. That refuelling of only 240 gallons took two hours after the launch was got going, but this allowed us good time to entertain the Governor.

Bill Nielson[88], as a Qantas traffic expert, had come up to put things in order, and after doing a good job handed over to Doug Laurie[89], who then ran the station. Hodder, a Civil Aviation wireless engineer, had also come up with his gear to see that all important communications were maintained. I returned to Australia on the first eastbound service, leaving Dili on 21st January by the Cambria, Captain Tapp[90] in command. On reaching Sydney I got down to it and made a full report on Dili and conditions there and the urgent necessity for a greater Australian interest in such an impoverished near neighbour, urging that trade should be built up. For instance, Japan and the Netherlands Indies bought Portuguese Timor's two types of coffee, 'Arabian'[91] and 'Robusta', and why should not Australia come into the market? I described Dili in the May 1941 issue of the magazine Walkabout, and in fact wrote about it so thoroughly in various reports that I was told the information which I had supplied was used as a textbook by our Australian troops when they occupied Dili just prior to the Japanese onslaught.

Mr Menzies (as he was then) was Prime Minister at this time, and after supplying a considerable amount of useful information on Portuguese Timor I received the following telegram from him: SINCERELY GRATEFUL YOUR LETTER ON RECEIPT OF WHICH TOOK NECESSARY STEPS TO HAVE WHOLE MATTER CONSIDERED STOP WOULD VALUE YOUR CONTINUED INTEREST.[92]

The third Qantas flight to Dili arrived in Portuguese Timor on 17th January 1941. The G-AETV *Coriolanus* was flown by Captain H B Hussey.[93] The crew were once again had been approached by E A Crome and took with

[88]    William Paterson Nielson had been born in 1894 in Dumfries, Scotland, and moved to Adelaide, South Australia, from where he enlisted in the Royal Australian Air Force in September 1943.

[89]    Douglas Gwyn Laurie was born in 1911 at Fremantle, Western Australia, and served in the Royal Australian Air Force from July 1941 until February 1942.

[90]    Russell Brooke Tapp was born in 1898 and served as a Flight-Lieutenant with the Royal Australian Air Force during the Second World War.

[91]    East Timor still remains one of the dominant producers of arabica coffee, Mark Dodd, 'East Timor looks to coffee', *The Age* 26 December 2000, Business Section, p. 1.

[92]    Sir Hudson Fysh. *Qantas at War*, *op.cit.*, p. 114.

[93]    Captain Hussey had been born on 11th February 1896 at Port Elliot, South Australia, and had enlisted in the Royal Australian Air Force on 6th January 1921. He was to be involved in the saving of the Qantas Empire flying-boat Camilla during the Japanese bombing of Darwin in February 1942, Douglas Gillison, *Royal Australian Air Force 1939–1942*, Canberra: Australian War Memorial, 1962, p. 427.

84

him 54 postal covers, and brought back an additional 21, with the return journey piloted by R B Tapp. Some of the covers were addressed to Crome and others to Captain E C Johnston and Hudson Fysh, founder of Qantas. [94] There was yet another Qantas flight to Dili several days later, piloted by Captain Ormond Dare Denny[95].

With Qantas officially starting its service in January 1941, in the following month the Japanese made three survey flights over Dili from the Pelew Islands. The Portuguese complained but there was nothing more they could do.[96] Also soon afterwards a large quantity of meteorological equipment from Tokyo was brought to Dili to be delivered to the Japanese Consul. When the Portuguese Customs insisted on inspecting the packages, the Japanese Consul hastily claimed that there was some mistake and the consignment was not for him. The equipment was, nevertheless, impounded and was still there at the end of the year when the joint Australian-Dutch force arrived in East Timor.[97]

On the 13th April 1941 Ross was finally posted to Dili as 'Temporary Technical Representative, Department of Civil Aviation'. In essence he was Australia's unofficial representative in Portuguese Timor.

David Ross was born on 15th March 1902, and had joined the Royal Australian Navy at the age of thirteen, having won an Australia-wide scholarship to be a cadet midshipman at Jervis Bay. When he was nineteen, he was sent to Britain and spent three years on Royal Navy vessels until 1925 when he returned to Australia to train as a naval pilot at Point Cook, near Melbourne. In 1931 he had been transferred to the Civil Aviation Branch of the Department of Defence. Two years later he was involved in surveying a possible Singapore-Darwin air route for the Australian government and in 1934, as mentioned earlier, had taken part in the Adelaide-Brisbane Air Race. Ross then served as Chief Inspector, Flying Branch, Department of Civil Aviation, visiting Dili again in January 1941.

---

[94]    See Stanley Gibbons Australia. *Public Auction Sale, Saturday, October 24th, 1992*, Hawthorn, 1992, lots 548–49, illustrated; and various catalogues by Charles Leski & Associates.

[95]    Born on 13th May 1899 in Northcote, Melbourne, the son of H D Denny of 22 Smith St, Northcote, he was a coachbuilder and wheelwright and enlisted on 10th May 1918 in the 5th Bn, 1st AIF and had embarked on the SS *Carpentaria* on 7th November 1918, returning soon afterwards. He joined the Royal Australian Air Force on 5th September 1921. He became a Squadron Leader in RAAF Reserve during the Second World War.

[96]    *The Argus* 22 February 1941, p. 3.

[97]    Bernard Callinan, *op.cit.*, p. 20.

Bernard Callinan described Ross as 'a tall, lean, large-boned man'[98]. Patricio da Luz, a radio station operator in Dili, described Ross as 'a terrific mate. I [da Luz] was a single man then. David and I used to chase the girls and drink together. I learnt a lot of Australian tricks from him, all sorts of things, but specially how to swear.'[99]

The major official role for Ross was to oversee Qantas flights from Darwin to Batavia via Dili. However it was obvious to all, including the Japanese, what his real task was. Although he did not officially report to the Department of External Affairs, but to the Director-General of the Department of Civil Aviation, only eight days after he had arrived in Dili, Ross had been given a note 'Memorandum, by Safe Hand of Commander, Qantas Empire Airways, for Personal Delivery to Mr Ross Only'. It was marked 'Most Secret – destroy on receipt' and notified Ross that a civilian clerk, F J A Whittaker, would be appearing in Dili 'to assist you in carrying out your duties'. Paymaster-Lieutenant John Whittaker, a Naval Intelligence Officer, was born in Bucklow, Cheshire, England, and 'had many years experience in the Malay Archipelago and is well versed in the Malay tongue'. Bernard Callinan, who described him as a 'short red-faced man' openly wrote of him as an intelligence officer in *Independent Company*[100]. As Peter Hastings noted:

Thus Australia's first representation in Portuguese Timor – among the first of our foreign missions – initially comprised a political officer acting as a Civil Aviation Department technical representative assisted in turn by a clerk who was, in fact, a spy, a non-uniformed naval intelligence officer working on behalf of a belligerent in a neutral country.

In March and April 1941 Clement Hugh Archer from the British Consular Service was sent to Dili to draw up a report on East Timor, which he was to complete on 3rd May. Archer had joined the British Consular Service in 1919 when he took up a posting to Tokyo as Student Interpreter. After extensive service in Kobe, Yokohama and Tokyo, in 1934 he was made British Consul in Tamsui (Taipei) remaining there until early 1941 when all British Consular Staff in Formosa, then a part of the Japanese Empire, were

---

[98]    *ibid.*, p. 9.
[99]    Michele Turner, *Telling East Timor: Personal Testimonies 1942–1992*, Kensington, NSW: University of NSW Press, 1992, p. 7.
[100]   ibid, p. 14.

expelled. Archer continued on to Australia where he wrote up his long report on the Japanese presence in East Timor prior to being posted to Tahiti in September 1941. Certainly the British were expecting some Japanese moves in the Pacific – on 17th April 1941 the British government had issued a Board of Trade order, coming into force on 30th April, enforcing export controls to Timor, Macao and Thailand.

On 14th October 1941 the Japanese government finally announced that they had been granted permission to fly from Palau to Dili. Japan was also able to establish direct mail links with East Timor. Two days later the Australian government told the press that they had delayed the visit of R G Casey, Australian Minister to the United States, to Australia so that he could conduct important discussions with the Americans.[101]

A month before Ross was appointed, in March 1941 the Australian government decided to prepare for the deployment of a force of 1200 men at Kupang in Dutch-controlled West Timor. Edmund Lind, a doctor and officer in the First World War, was sent to Timor to draw up logistics plans (he was to die from a heart attack on 2nd May 1944). After years of prevarication, Ross was finally appointed Consul on 10th December, two days after the Pacific War began.

*The Argus* noted on 19th December 1941:

Sleepy Portuguese Timor, least of the possessions in Lisbon's 'courtesy empire' has become by the irony of war a new focal point for the world's attention. It is not for its own sake that people in London or Tokio, or even Lisbon, are interested in this one-horse colony – except that it shows signs of containing some 'liquid gold'.

Timor's petrol remains only a possibility; its present interest lies in the fact that it bridges the gap between the Netherlands East Indies to the north and Darwin only 400 miles away to the south. And being in the hands of a powerless Power, it could be used like other harmless neutrals which find themselves in the firing line…

Dili itself, which bears the proud title of capital, is a sleepy little seaside village with a few shops sprawling along the seafront, and a backing of picturesque mammoth trees which are used for mooring the Dutch packets which connect it with the outside world.

---

[101]    *The Times* 15 October 1941, p. 3; 17 October 1941, p. 3 & 4; Robert M Spaulding, 'Japanese Airmail to Saipan, Palau and Portuguese Timor', *Japanese Philately* (June 1985).

Before the coming of Qantas, a year or so ago, it was Dili's only connection. The E and A shops once called here. Burns, Philp once called there. But it didn't pay. When the Japanese arranged to send a special air service for the convenience of the Dili folk, nobody was deceived for a moment.

Only a few hundred Portuguese maintain their authority over the colony's 400,000 one-time headhunters. Administration is in the hands of colonial military officers ranging from majors to corporals who govern a chain of circumscriptions of tax-gathering units. Their administration is neither harsh nor progressive. It extends to very little beyond extracting from the natives a head tax which goes into a general fund for paying officials' salaries – sooner or later. There is a case on record of an official who was 4 years in arrears with his pay envelope.

Australians who have visited the island find a touch of opera bouffe about all its administration and there is a chronic lack of money in this poorest of Portugal's poor colonial relations. It is said that jungle tribes who are brought in to Dili in accordance with an ordinance requiring them to lend a hand in street-sweeping have sometimes to be paid in postage stamps! When the Portuguese decided to go in for olive-oil production, they bought the pressing machinery first, and then planted the trees.

What wealth the colony has, actual or potential, is scattered over the jumble of mountains which form the backbone of the island and the extensive plain stretching to the southern shore. On the uplands grows the arabica coffee, producing a small bean and a relatively light crop, but ranking among the world's finest coffees. In times of peace most of it went to Macassar or to distant Stockholm, where they have a taste for good coffee.

But it is the coastal plain, with its wide swamps and masses of impenetrable canegrass, which has attracted most attention. For 20 or 30 years Australian investors have been making spasmodic attempts to discover oil in commercial quantities in Australian-owned concessions, particularly toward the eastern tip of the island. Extravagant surface evidence of the existence of oil has been found in seepage and exuberant emissions of gas. Attempts by Australian companies to exploit the undoubted petroleum resources of the island, however, have met with obstacles – largely political.

Dr Arthur Wade, a member of the recent Commonwealth Oil Advisory Committee, held a high opinion of the petroleum potential of the island, particularly along the south coast facing Australia.

Otherwise the colony produces little except native crops. Manganese and gold have been found here and there but there is no active production of commercial minerals. Communications are primitive. There are no navigable waterways; the rivers rush down to the shore in summer torrents and dry away after the rains.

Many visitors to the colony have wondered why the Portuguese clung to it when they had the large African possessions of Angola and Mozambique to develop. One reason may be that official salaries, by some obscure regulation, are paid in patagas, or Mexican dollars, instead of the escudo. Since these have not depreciated so heavily, salaries are worth several times their nominal value – when they are paid.

But the real reason has probably been one of prestige. Living so largely on their grandiose past, the Portuguese cling to the memory of their 'antepassados' the forebears who carved out an empire which was defined by Papal decree as covering one-half of the globe. To toss away even a useless fragment of what is left might set a bad precedent. But to defend it adequately would be a sheer impossibility.[102]

Since 1940 Australia had the task of providing reinforcements for the Dutch in West Timor[103], but also seems to have had the responsibility, in time of war, to prevent the Japanese from taking East Timor.[104] A week after Ross finally became Consul, a combined Australian-Dutch force men arrived in East Timor nominally to protect the place from attack by the Japanese – the last Qantas flight had been on 6th December. The Australian government felt that the Portuguese troops there were 'unlikely to provide [an] adequate or effective defence'[105]. The Portuguese governor fled to the hills and refused the protection of the allied forces. However he eventually acceded to their demands and the Allies ran an uneasy but not opposed occupation until the arrival of the Japanese in February 1942.

Arthur Staughton died in 1949. The Concession was deemed to have lapsed and no significant oil was found on land in East Timor. Interestingly, during the war, Stuart St Clair, writing in *National Geographic Magazine* in 1943, did highlight the presence of natural gases.[106] Nothing came of the troubles

---

[102]   *The Argus* 19 December 1941, p. 4.
[103]   W D McIntyre, *The Singapore Naval Base*, London: Macmillan, 1979, p. 177.
[104]   *ibid*, p. 174.
[105]   Cited in David Day, *The Great Betrayal: Britain, Australia & the Onset of the Pacific War 1939–42*, North Ryde, NSW: Angus & Robertson, 1988, p. 242.
[106]   Stuart St Clair, 'Timor: a key to the Indies', *National Geographic Magazine* (Sept 1943), p. 366. His keen interest in oil could have come from his background in

that had plagued East Timor throughout the 1910s, 1920s and 1930s – its possible sale to another power, and the search for oil – until the Indonesian annexation in 1975. However considerable holdings of oil were later found in the seas around Timor in the 1980s, the discoveries forming the basis of the Timor Gap Treaty of 1989. Australia signed a revised Timor Gap Treaty covering oil in the seas south of East Timor as it became independent on 20th May 2002.

engineering, see *Who's Who in Engineering* and the *Encyclopedia of American Biography*.

# BIBLIOGRAPHY

Australian Archives.
*The Age* (Melbourne).
*The Argus* (Melbourne).
*The Times* (London).

*Australian Dictionary of Biography.*
*Dictionary of National Biography.*
*Dictionary of New Zealand Biography*, online edition.
*Oxford Dictionary of National Biography.*
*Who's Who* (London).
*Who's Who in Australia.*
*Who's Who in Engineering*, New York: John W Leonard Corporation 1922.

Arndt, H W. 'Goa and East Timor: Contrasting Histories', *Quadrant* (July-August 2001), pp. 26–28.

Begg, A C & Begg, N C. *The world of John Boultbee.* Christchurch: Whitcoulls, 1979.

Bessa, Carlos. 'Le Portugal Neutre: la seconde guerre mondiale 1939–1945' [Neutral Portugal in World War II], *Guerres Mondiales et Conflits Contemporains* Vol 45, no 178 (1995), pp. 43-65.

Boultbee, John. *Journal of a rambler* edited by June Starke, Auckland: Oxford University Press, 1986.

Boxer, C R. 'Portuguese Timor: a rough island story, 1515–1960', *History Today* Vol 10, no 5 1960, pp. 349-55.

Caldwell, Malcolm. 'Oil and imperialism in East Asia', *Journal of Contemporary Asia* Vol 1, no 3 (1971), pp. 4–35.

Callinan, Bernard. *Independent Company*, London: Heinemann, 1953.

Cobham, Alan. *Australia and Back*, London: A&C Black, 1926.

Cook, Chris. *Sources in British Political History 1900–1951*, London: Macmillan, 1975.

Craigie, Sir Robert. *Behind the Japanese Mask*, London: Hutchinson, 1945.

Crittenden, Victor. *A bibliography of the First Fleet*, Canberra: Australian National University, 1981.

Currey, Charles H. *The transportation, escape and pardoning of Mary Bryant*, Sydney: Angus & Robertson 1963.

Davidson, Katherine Georgina. The Portuguese Colonisation of Timor: the final stage 1850–1912, PhD Thesis, University of New South Wales 1995.

Day, David. *The Great Betrayal: Britain, Australia & the Onset of the Pacific War 1939-42*, North Ryde, NSW: Angus & Robertson, 1988.

Debenham, Frank. *Nyasaland: the land of the lake*, London: HMSO, 1955.

*Documents on Australian Foreign Policy*, Canberra: AGPS 1975-, 9 Vols.

Dunn, James. *Timor: a people betrayed*, Sydney: ABC Books 2001.

Dunn, James. *East Timor: a rough passage to independence*, Double Day, NSW: Longueville Books, 2003.

Edwardes, Michael. *Ralph Fitch, Elizabethan in the Indies*, London: Faber, 1972.

*Encyclopedia of American Biography*, New York: Harper & Row, 1974.

Erickson, Carolly. *The Girl from Botany Bay: the true story of the convict Mary Broad and her extraordinary escape*, Sydney: Macmillan, 2004.

Eustis, Nelson. *The Greatest Air Race: England – Australia 1919*, Adelaide: Rigby, 1994.

Eustis, Nelson (ed). *The Australian Air Mail Catalogue*, Adelaide: Hobby Investments, 2002.

Flinders, Matthew. *A Voyage to Terra Australia*, London, 1814, Vol 1.

Frei, Henry P. 'Japan's reluctant decision to occupy Portuguese Timor, 1 January 1942 – 20 February 1942', *Australian Historical Studies* Vol 27, No 107 (1996), pp. 281–302.

Freycinet, Louis de. *Reflections on New South Wales 1788–1839*, Potts Point, NSW: Hordern House 2001.

Fysh, Sir Hudson. *Qantas at War*, Sydney: Angus & Robertson, 1968.

Gallagher, Tom. 'Anglo-Portuguese relations since 1900', *History Today* (June 1986), pp. 42-46.

Gammage, Bill. 'Early boundaries of New South Wales', *Historical Studies* Vol 19, No 77 (1981), pp. 524–31.

Gillen, Mollie. *The Founders of Australia*, North Sydney: Library of Australian History, 1989.

Gillison, Douglas. *Royal Australian Air Force 1939–1942*, Canberra: Australian War Memorial, 1962.

Great Britain. *The Foreign Office List, and Diplomatic and Consular Year Book for 1941*, London: Harrison & Sons, 1941.

Gunn, Geoffrey C. *Timor Loro Sae: 500 years*, Macau: Livros do Oriente, 1999.

Gunn, Geoffrey C & Lee, Jefferson. *A Critical View of Western Journalism and Scholarship on East Timor*, Manila: Journal of Contemporary Asia, 1994.

Gwynn-Jones, Terry. *Pioneer Airwoman: the story of Mrs Bonney*, Adelaide: Rigby, 1979.

Hart, H G. *The Annual Army List and Militia List for 1860*, London: John Murray, 1860.

Hastings, Peter. 'Timor – some Australian attitudes 1903–1941', in James Cotton (ed), *East Timor & Australia*, Canberra 1999, Chapter 1.

Hughes, Robert. *The Fatal Shore*, London: Collins Harvill, 1987.

Johns, R K. *History and role of government geological surveys in Australia*, Adelaide: Government Printer, 1976.

King, Jonathan. *Mary Bryant: Her Life and Escape from Botany Bay*, Pymble, NSW: Simon & Schuster, 2004.

Kunio, Katayama. 'The expansion of Japanese Shipping into Southeast Asia before World War I: the Case of OSK', *Great Circle* Vol 8, no 1 (1986), pp. 13–26.

Leski, Charles & Associates Pty Ltd. *Airmail Auction*, 11 April 1989.

Leski, Charles & Associates Pty Ltd. *Airmails II Auction*, 10 December 1990.

Leski, Charles & Associates Pty Ltd. *Airmails III Auction*, 6 May 1991.

Leski, Charles & Associates Pty Ltd. *Airmails IV Auction*, 9 December 1992.

Leski, Charles & Associates Pty Ltd. *Airmails V Auction*, 19 November 1994.

Lombard-Jourdan, Anne. 'François Péron and Charles Lesueur a Timor: une chasse au crocodile en 1803', *Archipel* No 54 (1997), pp. 81–121.

Marchant, James. *Alfred Russel Wallace: Letters and Reminiscences*, New York: Arno Press, 1975.

Marden, Luis. 'Wreck of HMS Pandora', *National Geographic Magazine* Vol 168, no 4 (October 1985), pp. 422-51.

McIntyre, W D. *The Singapore Naval Base*, London: Macmillan, 1979.

Murray, Robert. 'Shell at War', *Quadrant* (December 2001), pp. 49-55.

Nicholson, Ian Hawkins. *Gazetteer of Sydney Shippings 1788–1840*, Canberra: Roebuck, 1981.

'Oil explorers embark on a new drilling adventure to end the mysteries in the Timor Gap', *Petroleum Gazette* (1992), No 2, pp. 23-42.

Pottle, Frederick Albert. *Boswell and the Girl from Botany Bay*, London: Heinemann, 1938.

'Production sharing regime poses new challenges for Timor Sea explorers', *Petroleum Gazette* (1995), No 1, pp. 13–17.

Rawson, Geoffrey. *The strange case of Mary Bryant*, London: Robert Hale, 1938.

Rayner, Robert J. *The Army and the Defence of Darwin Fortress*, Sydney: Rudder Press, 1995.

Rose, Lyndon. *Richard Siddins of Port Jackson*, Canberra: Roebuck Books, 1984.

St Clair, Stuart. 'Timor: a key to the Indies', *National Geographic Magazine* (September 1943), pp. 355-84.

Sayers, C E. *By These We Flourish: a history of Warrnambool*, Melbourne: Heinemann, 1969.

Shorten, Ann R. 'The Australian Maritime Tradition: the letters of Clive Henderson 1922–1924', *Great Circle* Vol 8, no 1 (1986), pp. 1–12.

Souter, Gavin. *Company of Heralds*, Carlton: Melbourne University Press, 1981.

Sowash, William Burton. 'Colonial rivalries in Timor', *The Far Eastern Quarterly* Vol 7, no 3 (May 1948), pp. 227–35.

Spaulding, Robert M. 'Japanese Airmail to Saipan, Palau and Portuguese Timor', *Japanese Philately* (June 1985).

Steven, Margaret. *Merchant Campbell 1769–1846*, Melbourne: Oxford University Press, 1965.

Stone, Glyn. *The Oldest Ally: Britain and the Portuguese Connection 1936–1941*, London: The Royal Historical Society, 1994.

Tarling, Nicholas. 'Britain, Portugal and East Timor in 1941', *Journal of Southeast Asian Studies* Vol 27, no 1 (1996), pp. 132–38.

Timor Oil. *Petroleum Oil: the history of oil exploration in the island of Timor, prepared from the records of various companies in New South Wales (Australia); together with several experts' reports made in connection therewith*, Sydney: Timor Oil Ltd, 1932.

*Voyage autour du monde*, Paris 1844.

White, Ken. *Criado: a story of East Timor*, Briar Hill, Vic: Indra Publishing, 2002.

Wilson, John G. *The forgotten naturalist: in search of Alfred Russel Wallace*, Melbourne: Australian Scholarly Publishing, 2000.

Wray, Christopher. *Timor 1942: Australian Commandos at war with the Japanese*, Melbourne: Hutchinson, 1987.

# INDEX

Fitzmaurice, Henry (1886–1952),
British Consul-General in Batavia,
73
Fitzmaurice, Rev Sir Henry (1886–
1952), British Consul-General in
Batavia 1931–39, 68
Flinders, Matthew (1774–1814),
Australian explorer, 11, 13
Fogasa, Jorge, Portuguese sailor, 5
Forbes, Henry Ogg (1851–1932),
Scottish scientist and Australian
explorer, 20
Foxall (née Dobbie), Margaret
Nerissa, 38
Foxall, Edward William (d. 1926), 38
Foxall, Henry George (1884–1966),
Australian engineer, 37, 38, 43, 45,
51, 52, 58
Foxall, John Stewart (1887–1967),
Australian engineer, 38
Freycinet, Louis-Claude Desaules de
(1779–1842), French cartographer,
12
Freycinet, Rose (1794–1832), French
diarist, 12
Fysh, Sir Wilmot Hudson (1895–
1974), Australian airline director,
74, 76, 81

**G**

Garmston, Samuel (1788–1859),
British army officer, 8
Geach, – (fl 1861), British mining
engineer in Dili, 14, 15, 16, 17, 18
Godinho de Erédia, Manuel (1563–
1623), Portuguese author, 6
Graham, Sir James (1856–1913),
Australian physician and
politician, 37
Graham, Sir Ronald William (1870–
1949), British diplomat, 33, 34
Green, -, manager at Pualaca, 50

**H**

Hart, – (fl 1861), English resident of
Dili, 14, 15, 17
Hastings, Peter Dunstan (1920–
1990), Australian journalist,
academic and commentator, 85
Heath, – (d. 1898), Royal Navy
midshipman, 22
Helms, – (fl 1901), Australian ship
captain, 23
Henley, Sir Thomas (1860–1935),
Australian politician and builder,
56
Herman, Samuel (1795–1879),
Jewish scholar and minister, 20
Higgs, William Guy (1862–1951),
Australian Politician, 27
Hodder, – (fl 1941), Australian
wireless engineer, 83
Houghton, -, American financier, 68
Hussey, Herbert Brindley (1896–
1958), Royal Australian Air Force
Officer, 83

**I**

Ingley, – (d. 1912), Portuguese Army
Officer, 28

**J**

Jacobs, Samuel Joshua (1853–1937),
Australian businessman, 64
Jeffrey, E F (fl 1923), Royal Navy
Officer, 34
Jellicoe, John Rushworth, 1st Earl
(1859–1935), British Admiral, 62
Johnston, E C (1896–1988),
Australian pilot, 75, 76, 84

**K**

Karnebeek, Herman Adriaan van
(1874–1942), Dutch Foreign
Minister 1918–27, 34
Kent, Duke of, George (1902–1942),
2

www.ingramcontent.com/pod-product-compliance
Lightning Source LLC
Chambersburg PA
CBHW060754100426